A BENN STUDY · DRAMA

THE NEW MERMAIDS

The Man of Mode

The Man of Mode

SIR GEORGE ETHEREGE

Edited by

JOHN BARNARD

Professor of English Literature
University of Leeds

LONDON/ERNEST BENN LIMITED

NEW YORK/W. W. NORTON AND COMPANY INC.

First published in this form 1979
by Ernest Benn Limited
25 New Street Square, Fleet Street, London EC4A 3JA
& Sovereign Way, Tonbridge, Kent TN9 1RW

© *Ernest Benn Limited 1979*

Published in the United States of America by
W. W. Norton and Company Inc.
500 Fifth Avenue, New York, N.Y. 10036

Distributed in Canada by
The General Publishing Company Limited, Toronto

Printed in Great Britain

British Library Cataloguing in Publication Data

Etherege, *Sir* George
    The man of mode. – (New mermaids).
    I. Title   II. Barnard, John Michael   III. Series
    822'.4   PR3432

ISBN 0–510–33500–4   Pbk.
ISBN 0–393–90041–X   (U.S.A.)

CONTENTS

ACKNOWLEDGEMENTS

IN PREPARING THIS EDITION my greatest debt has been to the play's earlier editors. H. F. B. Brett-Smith's learned annotation and careful handling of textual difficulties helped at crucial points. John Conaghan's Fountainwell text, which contains the fullest bibliographical examination yet published of *The Man of Mode*'s first edition, was helpful in preparing both text and commentary. In modernizing, A. W. Verity's edition gave help on some occasions. The sane, informed, and careful scholarship of W. B. Carnochan's Regents Restoration edition was constantly of use.

With real generosity, Professor Harold Brooks allowed the use of unpublished information from his edition of Oldham—so enabling Dorimant's reference to an elephant, which has defeated previous editors, to be revealed as a topical allusion. Paul Levy gave gastronomic advice. Mr Philip Wilby of the University of Leeds very kindly created modern versions of Dr Staggins's contemporary setting of Dorimant's song ('When first Amintas') and of Sir Car Scroope's song, and did so at very short notice.

Mr David Masson of the Brotherton Collection, the University of Leeds, was uniformly patient and obliging, as were the staff of the Bodleian Library, Mr Robert Kenedy of the Victoria and Albert Museum, and Dr R. A. Sayce, Librarian of Worcester College, Oxford. For her advice on the Introduction I am deeply indebted to Hermione Lee of the University of York. Both the General Editor of this volume, Dr Brian Gibbons, and my publisher, John Collis, generously gave minute attention to the text and Introduction, saving me from slips and errors of various kinds, and suggested several improvements. I must also thank Paddy Rowe and Sara Broadbent for their care and expertise with an often difficult task in preparing the typescript.

Denton   J.B.
October 1978

INTRODUCTION

THE AUTHOR

ACCORDING TO WILLIAM OLDYS, Sir George Etherege's birth took place in 1636: if so, he cannot have been born until after the summer of that year. He was the eldest son, but not the eldest child, of the seven children of Captain George Etherege (b. 1607) and Maria Powney.[1] The family was prosperously middle-class. The dramatist's grandfather, also named George (1576–1658), called himself a gentleman, and was a successful vintner and a shareholder in the Virginia and Bermuda Companies, sufficiently well-to-do to move from London to Bray, near Maidenhead, some time after 1628. In the same year as the future playwright's probable birth, Etherege's father purchased the post of purveyor to Queen Henrietta Maria, a court office 'worth about two hundred pounds per annum before the troubles'.[2] The Civil War, however, disrupted any career within the Court. Captain George Etherege followed the Queen to France after her escape in 1644. He died there in 1650, leaving his children to be supported by their grandfather.

Etherege's letters indicate that he had a reasonable education. Although there is no firm evidence to support the tradition that he attended Lord Williams's Grammar School at Thame with Antony à Wood, he was well-read in English poetry, had at least a working knowledge of Horace (despite Dennis's assertion that he knew 'neither Latin nor Greek'), and was fluent in French. He may also have travelled in France and Flanders during his youth, but by 1654 was apprenticed to an attorney at Beaconsfield, George Gosnold, to whom he was still articled in August 1658.

The transformation of an articled clerk into a wit and associate of young aristocrats had taken place by winter of 1663–64 when he carried on a bawdy verse correspondence with Lord Buckhurst, to

[1] The sources for Etherege's life, together with some new evidence, are brought together in the Introduction to the *Letters of Sir George Etherege*, ed. Frederick Bracher (Berkeley, Los Angeles, London, 1974). Further, see the articles cited there; William Oldys's account in *Biographica Britannica*, vol. 3 (1750), 1841, the Introduction to H. F. B. Brett-Smith's edition of *The Dramatic Works of Sir George Etherege* (Oxford, 1927), and *The Letterbook of Sir George Etherege*, ed. Sybil Rosenfeld (1927).
[2] Eleanore Boswell, 'Sir George Etherege', *Review of English Studies*, vol. 7 (1931), 207; Dorothy Foster, ibid., vol. 8 (1932), 459.

whom his first play, *The Comical Revenge* (1664), is dedicated. Etherege was by then approaching thirty, and, like many a man whose family had suffered for its Royalist sympathies (though the Etheregees appear to have suffered a good deal less than some), the obvious course of advancement was through noble, preferably royal, patronage. By the time his second play, *She Wou'd if She Cou'd*, was acted four years later, he was a member of the group of courtiers, wits, and rakes which included Sir Charles Sedley, the Earl of Rochester, and the Duke of Buckingham.

Etherege's easy wit and literary success brought court favour. In 1668 he was made Gentleman of the Privy Chamber in Ordinary, and then appointed to an important and delicate diplomatic mission to Turkey as Sir Daniel Hervey's secretary. Returning to London in 1671, he once more took up the rakish life of a man about town. Not until 1676 was *The Man of Mode* produced, and by then, according to the Dedication, Etherege was in some way in the service of Mary of Modena, wife of the future James II, brother of the King. That summer, after the success of his comedy, Etherege was involved in the notorious episode of Rochester's scouring of the watch at Epsom. Although the playwright tried to act as peacemaker, one of the party was seriously injured: on 29 June Charles Hatton reported:

> Mr Downs is dead. Y^e Ld Rochester doth abscond, and soe doth Etheridge, and Capt Bridges who ocasioned ye riot Sunday sennight. They were tossing some fidlers in a blanket for refusing to play, and a barber, upon ye noise, going to see what ye matter, they seized upon him, and, to free himself from them, he offered to carry them to ye handsomest woman in Epsom, and directed them to the constables house, who demanding what they came for, they told him a wh..., and, he refusing to let them in, they broke open his doores and broke his head, and beate him very severely. At last, he made his escape, called his watch, and Etheridge made a submissive oration to them and soe far appeased them that ye constable dismissed his watch. But presently after, ye Ld Rochester drew upon ye constable. Mr Downs, to prevent his pass, seized upon him, ye constable cryed out murther, and, the watch returning, one came behind Mr Downs and with a sprittle staff cleft his scull. Y^e Ld Rochester and ye rest run away, and Downs, having noe sword, snatched up a sticke and striking at them, they run him into ye side wth a half pike, and soe bruised his arm y^t he wase never able to stir it after.[3]

This episode does little credit to anyone involved except the watch, but it is worth quoting at length since it contrasts sharply with the claims for Dorimant's gentility within *The Man of Mode*. It is also

[3] *Correspondence of the Family of Hatton ...*, ed. E. M. Thompson, Camden Society, vol. 1 (1878), 133–4.

important to note that Etherege was about forty at the time, while Rochester was in his late twenties. None of this, however, affected Etherege's habits: in 1677 he was involved in a tavern squabble in which Fleetwood Shepherd was 'runn with a sword under the eye'.[4]

By 1679 the dramatist had gained both a knighthood and a wife, Mary Sheppard Arnold. Gildon's assertion that 'for Marrying a Fortune he was Knighted'[5] was seen very differently by contemporary satirists, who claim that he had married an ugly, old, rich woman for money, and in 1683 he is said to have been gaming away her money at Locket's.[6] It is difficult to distinguish truth from venomous rumour, but Etherege's extant letters to his wife are notably brief and usually concerned with money: he also refers to playing and losing at the Duchess of Mazarin's basset-table, probably during these years.

When James II became King in 1685, Etherege was again appointed to a diplomatic post, and left London with an eagerness which suggests that he was escaping from something. His letters written while Resident at Ratisbon give the most graphic account available of Etherege.[7] They reveal a lonely man, ill-adapted to the provincial formality and protocol of the envoys to the Diet. They also reveal a wry wit, coupled with a striking *insouciance*, which, in a diplomat, amounted to indiscretion. By 1685 the Diet of the Holy Roman Empire had lost most of its importance, and Etherege's essential duties were those of an observer of the uneasy truce preceding the War of the League of Augsburg. Etherege, bored and missing the delights of London, failed to establish proper relations with other envoys, while his card-playing and an affair with an itinerant actress caused considerable scandal. By the end of his first year he 'was practically a social outcast. He reacted by becoming all the more arrogant in his official capacity and apparently more dissolute in his private life.'[8] Yet the letters show another side of Etherege, one not incompatible with his impatience of formality—and with his failure to realize for some time that his secretary was sending adverse and maliciously detailed reports of his behaviour back to London while undercutting his position at Ratisbon. To a friend he wrote:

> I need not tell you I am good-natur'd. I who have forgiven so many
> Mistresses who have been false to me can well forgive a friend who has

---

[4] *Historical Manuscripts Commission, Calendar of the Manuscripts of the Marquis of Bath*, vol. 2 (1907), 160.

[5] Charles Gildon, *Lives and Characters of the English Dramatick Poets* [1699], p. 53.

[6] Thomas Wood, *Juvenalis Redivivum* (1683), p. 17.

[7] See the editions by Rosenfeld and Bracher cited above.

[8] *Letters of Sir George Etherege*, ed. Bracher, p. xx.

onely been negligent. My heart was never touch'd for any for whom
there remains not still some impression of kindness.[9]

This is more than the 'open-handedness' of the reprobate, for it is
based on a knowledge of the ways of the world and the heart. And
his temper is sceptical rather than cynical or atheistic:

I have ever enjoy'd a liberty of opinion in matters of Religion. 'Tis
indifferent to me whether there be an other in the world who thinks as I
do. This makes me have no temptation to talk of the business, but
quietly following the light within me, I leave that to them who were born
with the ambition of becoming Prophets or Legislators.[10]

'Good-nature' of this complexion was hardly likely to be
appreciated by any but a few in Ratisbon. Not until the spring of
1687 did Etherege realize the seriousness of his position. He then
turned his mind to business with an effectiveness which grew into
relish. But James's reign was already tottering. From midsummer
until November 1688 Etherege was rightly obsessed with the threat
of an invasion of England whose aim was to displace James II in
favour of William of Orange, though the evidence he sent to
London seems to have been taken less seriously than it ought.
Etherege's loyalty to James was a mixture of gratitude for past
favours and an emotional commitment to a concept of royalty sadly
out of touch with political reality. When in January 1689 Etherege
heard that James had reached Paris safely, he left Ratisbon to throw
in his lot with the Jacobites.

The tragi-comedy of these last years concludes in a mystery.
Etherege is not mentioned in the list of the Court in exile, so that he
may have arrived too late at St Germain to join the cause. Nor is it
certain when he died. Although his death probably took place in
May 1692, it was earlier reported in February 1691.[11] As a final
irony, the Benedictine monks at Ratisbon claimed that he died a
convert to Catholicism. Such a conversion would fit well with his
Jacobite sympathies, and would place Etherege, with Rochester, as
an aristocratic rake whose libertine mores finally concealed a conservative faith in hierarchy and a superstitious belief in religion. Or
it may be that he is another victim of the seventeenth-century
church's need to enforce the myth of 'surprising conversions'.

EARLY STAGE HISTORY AND RECEPTION

The first recorded performance of *The Man of Mode*, which may
also have been its premiere, was given before the King at the

[9] To Charles Boyle, 22 May 1687, ibid., p. 118.
[10] Unaddressed, 29 December 1687, ibid., p. 168.
[11] ibid., pp. xxiii–iv.

Duke's Theatre, Dorset Gardens, on 11 March 1676.[12] Although the company's move in 1672 to their new theatre, designed by Wren, had brought them closer to the City (near the Thames just south of Fleet Street), the King's presence at this early performance, Sir Car Scroope's prologue and song, Dryden's epilogue, and the eventual dedication to the Duchess of York, all proclaim the comedy's allegiance to the ethos and social assumptions surrounding the Court.

The Duke's Men, who had presented Etherege's two earlier plays, provided a strong cast. Thomas Betterton, famous for both his tragic roles and his portrayal of rake-heroes, took the part of Dorimant, while Mrs Barry, the tragic actress and one-time mistress of Rochester, may have played Mrs Loveit. The remainder of the cast offered more than effective support,[13] and in John Downes's professional judgement 'this Comedy being well Cloath'd and well *Acted*, got a great deal of Money'.[14] The 'extraordinary Success' of the production was long remembered.[15] Three days after the first recorded performance, a contemporary witness reported, 'This Sr Fopling makes at present all the discourse, to discover the persons meant by it',[16] an account supported many years later by John Dennis. Identifications varied wildly. At least one member of the audience identified Dorimant with the Duke of Monmouth '& his intrigue with Moll Kirke, Mrs Needham, & Lady Harriott Wentworth'.[17] The most common identification, however, was with Rochester:

> I remember very well that upon the first acting this Comedy, it was ... unanimously agreed, that [Dorimant] had in him several of the qualities of *Wilmot* Earl of *Rochester*, as, his Wit, his amorous Temper, the Charms that he had for the fair Sex, and his Inconstancy; the agreeable Manner of his chiding his Servants, which the late Bishop of *Salisbury*

[12] 'His Ma^{ts} Bill from His Royall Highnesse Theatre', dated 29 June 1676, P.R.O., L.C. 5/142, p. 1 (cited by Allardyce Nicoll, *A History of English Drama*, vol. 1, *Restoration Drama 1660–1700* (4th edn., Cambridge, 1952), 348). The King also attended a performance in April and took a 'Box for the Mayds of Hono^r'.

[13] John Downes, *Roscius Anglicanus* (1708), p. 36, gives the cast as:Dorimant—Betterton; Medley—Harris; Sir Fopling—Smith; Old Bellair—Leigh; Young Bellair—Jevon; Loveit—Mrs Barry; Bellinda—Mrs Betterton; Lady Woodvill—Mrs Leigh; Emilia—Mrs Twiford. J. H. Wilson, however, thinks that the role was created by Mary Lee, and only given to Mrs Barry after Mrs Lee's retirement in 1685 (*All the King's Ladies* (Chicago, 1958), p. 111).

[14] ibid.

[15] Charles Gildon, op. cit., p. 53.

[16] Peter Killigrew to his sister, 14 March; quoted in Joseph Spence, *Observations, Anecdotes, and Characters of Books and Men*, ed. James M. Osborn (Oxford, 1966), vol. 2, 638.

[17] ibid.

takes Notice of in his Life; and lastly, his repeating, on every Occasion, the Verses of *Waller*, for whom that noble Lord had a very particular Esteem.[18]

Dryden, though, is surely right to deny that any individual was hunted from the herd, and it is mistaken to search for any *à clef* pattern.[19] What is important is that the comic truthfulness of the play's representation of contemporary life was at once recognized. Sir Fopling quickly became a byword, and, more surprisingly, both Dorimant and Sir Fopling appear in a theological dispute in the same year.[20]

Unfortunately, records of performances in the seventeenth century are fragmentary.[21] *The Man of Mode* still enjoyed the Court's favour when it was performed at Whitehall in 1685 'with the usuall applause', and it was put on in Edinburgh, possibly in 1679 or 1680, by a group of actors who had broken away from the King's Men, led by Clarke and Goodman, and then by Haines.[22] There is

[18] John Dennis, *A Defense of Sir Fopling Flutter* (1722), in *The Critical Works of John Dennis*, ed. E. N. Hooker (Baltimore, Md., 1939–43), vol. 2, 248. Dean Lockier also identified Dorimant with Rochester in 1730; see Joseph Spence, *Anecdotes*, ed. cit., No. 638. The other main sources for contemporary identifications are Peter Killigrew (cited above); John Bowman (1651–1739), who was William Oldys's informant for his article in *Biographica Britannica* (vol. 3 (1750), 1841); the information given by Charles Sackville's descendants to Thomas Davies (*Dramatic Miscellanies* (1784), vol. 3, 169–70); and the testimony falsely ascribed to St Évremond in the 1707 edition of Rochester. In addition, the anonymous writer of *Poeta De Tristibus* (1681) thought Sir Fopling a self-portrait (Harold Love, 'The Satirised Characters in *Poeta De Tristibus*', *Philological Quarterly*, vol. 47 (1968), 553). Excluding St Évremond, the identifications are as follows: Dorimant = Rochester (Dennis, Lockier, Bowman), Monmouth (Killigrew), Dorset and Rochester (Sackville family); Harriet = Harriet Wentworth (Killigrew); Mrs Loveit = Moll Kirke (Killigrew); Bellinda = Mrs Needham (Killigrew); Sir Fopling = Edward Villiers (Killigrew), 'Beau' Hewitt (Bowman), Etherege (*Poeta De Tristibus*); Medley = Etherege (Bowman; Sir Charles Sedley has also been suggested as a possible model by later writers).

[19] But see J. M. Auffret, '*The Man of Mode* and *The Plain Dealer*: Common Origin and Parallels', *Études anglaises*, vol. 19 (1966), 209–22, who attempts to prove that Moll Kirke is 'the common origin of both comedies'. He further makes the interesting suggestion that the model for Sir Fopling was Charles Mordaunt, who was connected with the Duchess of York.

[20] Andrew Marvell, *Mr Smirke: or, the Divine in Mode* . . . (1676), cited in *Dramatic Works of Sir George Etherege*, ed. Brett-Smith, vol. 1, xxvi n.

[21] Further see *The London Stage 1660–1800*, ed. W. Van Lennep, E. L. Avery, A. H. Scouten, G. W. Stone, and C. B. Hogan, 11 vols. (Carbondale, Ill., 1960–68).

[22] Charles, Earl of Middleton, writing to Etherege on 7 December 1685 (*Letters*, ed. Bracher, p. 269), reported the success at Court. For the Edinburgh performance, see John Conaghan, 'A Prompt Copy of Etherege's *Man of Mode*', *Library Review*, vol. 21 (1968), 387–8.

some evidence to suggest that Etherege's comedy, along with *The Plain-Dealer*, temporarily lost favour in the public theatre in the late 1680s, and lay 'untouch'd and unsought-for' while lesser plays succeeded.[23] In 1693 the play was reprinted, and a revival was probably staged, a supposition supported by a cast list in a Harvard copy of the play. There was sufficient interest to justify a *Collected Works* in 1704.

Looking back in 1722, John Dennis claimed that the comedy had been 'well receiv'd, and believ'd by the people of *England* to be the most agreeable Comedy for about Half a Century'.[24] That claim needs to be seen in its context. Dennis's *Defense of Sir Fopling Flutter* is a deliberate reply to the covert Whig attack, mounted by Addison and Steele in the *Spectator*, which sought to discredit the Stuarts by attacking the immorality of the period's drama. The immediate cause of Dennis's pamphlet was the rehearsal of Steele's *The Conscious Lovers*, which was both bourgeois and Whig in its sympathies. At root, the argument, though coloured by political considerations, was an aesthetic confrontation over the nature of comedy. Steele believed in exemplary comedy while Dennis's classical theory of ridicule, finding its origins in Aristotle, was doomed to failure with the later eighteenth-century audience. Although Walpole in 1775 or 1776 thought *The Man of Mode* 'our first genteel comedy',[25] by that time the play had virtually disappeared from the stage, driven out by a changed public taste which insisted that its stage be 'moral'.

THE PLAY

There ought to be no question that *The Man of Mode* is a finely balanced and brilliantly executed comedy of the sexes, and that its psychological insight is allied to a complex and open exploration of the patterns and social proscriptions which, self-consciously and unconsciously, govern courtship. The conventions may differ from those of Shakespearean comedy or modern life, but the basic patterns (and human reasons for those patterns) remain constant. Courtship rituals are also games which are exploratory, allowing the lovers to discern the nature of their partner before full

[23] *The Lacedemonian Mercury*, 7 March 1692, cited in *The London Stage*. For the manuscript cast, which includes Betterton as Dorimant, Mrs Barry as Loveit, and Elinor Leigh as Lady Woodvill, see Edward A. Langhans, 'New Restoration Manuscript Casts', *Theatre Notebook*, vol. 27 (1972–73), 156–7.

[24] *A Defense of Sir Fopling Flutter*, ed. cit., vol. 2, 243.

[25] 'Thoughts on Comedy; Written in 1775 and 1776', *Works* (1798), vol. 2, 315.

commitment. As such they are at once defensive and offensive, creating room for both advance and retreat, and giving time for discrimination between the merely sexual and more lasting attractions. The norm from which the lovers start is inevitably supplied by their society, though usually the younger generation seeks its own pattern of conventions as distinct from that of their parents. *The Man of Mode* is about the enjoyable, necessary, and finally serious games which people play in the most crucial area in which personal fulfilment and instinctual drives have to be accommodated within a social framework—courtship and marriage. While it exhibits the tolerance and gaiety of comedy, *The Man of Mode* is not an entirely comforting or comfortable play. Its affirmation is balanced by an ironic scepticism.

A direct claim for the success and importance of Etherege's final comedy is necessary because interpretations vary so widely as to call any pretensions it may have to coherence or value into serious doubt. For Bonamy Dobrée, Etherege's three plays 'are pure works of art directed to no end but themselves' and are entirely unmotivated 'by any moral stimulus'. *The Man of Mode* has also been characterized as a 'delightfully satiric entertainment', as 'an uncompromisingly tough and realistic play', as a bleak and bitter comedy which exposes Dorimant's 'life of isolation', and as an expression of Dorimant's 'Hobbesian aggressiveness, competitiveness, and desire for power and "glory" . . . an egoistic assertion of self through control of others'.[26] This list by no means exhausts the possible interpretations, but is enough to suggest that the comedy's ambiguities arise either from the ingenuity of critics uneasily trying to answer L. C. Knights's case against Restoration comedy ('trivial, gross, and dull') or from the play's intrinsic resistance to the imposition of a single reading. If the latter, *The Man of Mode*'s refusal to lie comfortably within neatly woven analyses argues its claim to classic status in Frank Kermode's sense—that is, a work in which the multiplicity of what is signified is in excess of the signifier.

Part of the reason for the striking critical disparity is the com-

[26] Bonamy Dobrée, *Restoration Comedy* (Oxford, 1924), p. 60; Robert D. Hume, *The Development of English Drama in the Late Seventeenth Century* (Oxford, 1976), p. 97; Paul C. Davies, 'The State of Nature and the State of War: A Reconsideration of *The Man of Mode*', *University of Toronto Quarterly*, vol. 39 (1969), 53–62; Jocelyn Powell, 'George Etherege and the Form of a Comedy', *Restoration Theatre*, *Stratford-upon-Avon Studies 6*, ed. J. R. Brown and Bernard Harris (1965), p. 61; Dale Underwood, *Etherege and the Seventeenth Century Comedy of Manners* (New Haven, Conn., 1957), p. 73. For L. C. Knights's attack, see 'Restoration Comedy: The Reality and the Myth', *Explorations* (1946), pp. 131–49.

edy's own richness, but a too-frequent contributory factor is a
misunderstanding of how realistic comedy works, a misunderstanding of how such comedy, while needing to capture the texture
of a given society from a specific viewpoint, can nevertheless
transcend its period. There is a further associated unwillingness to
admit the way in which comedy's strongly formulaic patterns can
pose a serious examination of moral issues while appearing to
collapse those problems into the inevitable happy ending. In the
case of *The Man of Mode*, the episodic plot with its inclusion of Sir
Fopling, who is not strictly necessary but gives his name to the play
and rivals Dorimant in his appeal to the audience, provides an
additional difficulty.

The question of the delicate relationship between 'realism' and
comedy's bearing on actual life can be conveniently focussed on Sir
Fopling, Dorimant, Mrs Loveit, and Bellinda. J. H. Wilson argues
that Etherege's

> ... idealised portraits are recognisable as the patterns of mannered,
> aristocratic society. Here is no question of realism; Etherege seized
> upon and embodied in his play not the real, day by day life of Whitehall,
> but the life which Whitehall was pleased to imagine it led. Individual
> items may be factual, but the total picture is a comic illusion.[27]

But comic illusion does not exclude realism since 'realism' itself is a
literary convention. What matters is not that *The Man of Mode* is
selective, but that its enlarging and simplifying of contemporary
life is an interpretative act, which reveals the conflicting values
implicit in the tensions of the audience's experience. The early
evidence shows that the original audience was only too eager to
recognize its own world in the play. Sir Fopling, that is, offers the
classical Aristotelian pleasure of imitation (as do the marvellous
genre portraits of the Shoemaker and the Orange-woman). Laughter springs from instant recognizability, and from Etherege's pre-
cise observation of linguistic and social mannerisms. But the laughter at Sir Fopling also has its source in the audience's anxieties, as
Dryden was well aware:

> Yet every man is safe from what he feared,
> For no one fool is hunted from the herd.
>
> (Epilogue, 33–4)

Sir Fopling acts as a scapegoat for the audience's unadmitted fear
that it too may easily mistake form for substance, an anxiety
particularly alive in a period striving for a new style of sophistication. Dryden's efforts as critic and writer to establish 'correct'

---

[27] *The Court Wits* (Chicago, 1948), p. 164. Robert D. Hume cites this passage with
enthusiasm (op. cit., p. 91).

literary standards, Sprat and the Royal Society's efforts to create a concise and plain English, the life-style of Charles II's Court, and Wren's classicism, all owe something to an emulation of European civilization and culture. Curtis D. Cecil's study of the language of Restoration comedy makes clear the way in which the refinement of English prose style and the aspiration towards refined conversation were stimulated by European standards and, in particular, by the example of France.[28] A firm indicator of contemporary aspirations is apparent in the number of handbooks, frequently translated from the French, on manners and conversation published in these years. To the extent which French culture provided a standard, it also threatened cultural imperialism—the incidence in the play of words recently taken from the French is a lexical record of that influence. Hence the need to establish an English sophistication as distinct from the French in particular. Sir Fopling's inanities come from a passive acceptance of French values only equalled by his ignorance: he is a *Babu* Frenchman. Dorimant's style looks to France, and yet is distinctly English. It is very striking that when Sir Fopling reveals his ignorance by confusing the Comte de Bussy with Chapman's stage-hero (IV.i, 214–18), the laughter on stage assumes that everyone knows Bussy's *Histoire Amoureuse des Gaulles*, a witty, gossiping account of *liaisons* in aristocratic French society, as well as the names of famous French gallants and their valets. If this is a joke against Sir Fopling, it must also have been a joke which cut uncomfortably close for many in the audience: a knowledge of French gossip and books might be assumed in Charles II's Court, but hardly in the public theatre. The point is implied surely by Dryden's comment that 'Sir Fopling is a fool so nicely writ, /The ladies would mistake him for a wit . . .' (Epilogue, 7–8).

Taking Sir Fopling and Dorimant together it is evident that the audience is asked to split its knowledge of itself between the two. Sir Fopling exorcizes the fear that gallants may too often resemble his idiocies, while encouraging a covert admiration for the fearlessness of Dorimant's manipulation of the new style in manners. The simplicity of that division is, however, qualified by the suggestion that Dorimant, as much as Sir Fopling, may be no more than a man of mode. They are linked too in another way. Medley comments on his 'natural indulgence for fools' (III.ii, 128). The audience's

---

[28] ' "Une Espèce d'Éloquence Abrégée": the Idealised Speech of Restoration Comedy', *Études anglaises*, vol. 19 (1966), 15–25. See also Cecil's articles, 'Libertine and Précieux Elements in Restoration Comedy', *Essays in Criticism*, vol. 9 (1959), 239–51, and 'Raillery in Restoration Comedy', *Huntington Library Quarterly*, vol. 29 (1965–66), 147–59.

attitude to Sir Fopling is at once aggressive and tolerant, even affectionate. Aggression is there because Sir Fopling embodies anxieties, warmth because his monomania makes him indestructible. His complacency means that he is all essential self, and to a degree the invulnerability of his two-dimensional selfhood is enviable. The audience's natural indulgence for fools has a surprising relationship with its natural indulgence for the rake.

Both characters, then, give a significant reflection of contemporary mores in the London of the 1670s, a reflection which assumes the desirability of polished manners. That it reflects an aspiration rather than a fact is self-evident. Dorimant's 'genteel' and civil behaviour eschews brawls and whores: the life of Rochester and Etherege clearly did not. Nor does the play show any of the main characters pursuing a career at Court or elsewhere. It is also striking that although *The Man of Mode* implies the existence of a *demi-monde*, it mutes its appearance. Mrs Loveit is, says Dorimant, a 'person of quality' (III.ii, 217) as well as being the 'most noted coquette in town' (IV.i, 190). Both she and Bellinda move naturally in Lady Townley's world. On the other hand, when Dorimant directs suspicion away from Bellinda by pretending she is mercenary, he reminds the audience of the existence of kept women and whores in the town. Nell Gwynn was only the most obvious example of a woman who had succeeded in Charles's London. Moll Kirke, Maid of Honour to the Duchess of York, had a well-publicized affair first with the Duke of Monmouth and then with the Earl of Mulgrave in 1674–76. She was then rumoured to have married Lord Mordaunt, a noted fop, in Paris, but in fact ended as the wife of Sir Thomas Vernon in 1677.[29] Mrs Loveit's flirtation with Sir Fopling reflects a possible resolution to her ambiguous position in a world which is harsh to the woman whose reputation is threatened. Dorimant tells her that she has a moderate 'stock of reputation left yet' (V.i, 136–7). She must choose how best to use that stock. *The Man of Mode* needs to treat this area with dramatic tact. It might be said to glamorize the promiscuity of the town by passing over the figures of Bellinda and Mrs Loveit, but the audience also knew that in their society experienced women might attain considerable status and even power. That ambiguity is one which the play chooses not to explore, because it is finally a comedy of courtship. The audience's experience of actuality is brought to bear on the comic world, and tests its resolution. 'Realism' is inevitably selective. The morality of art does not lie in the creation of a system acceptable to a moral philosopher, but in its truth to the inconsistencies and contradictions of life experienced within a

[29] See J. M. Auffret, art. cit., pp. 215–16.

specific context, whose values may be radically confused. The moral conflicts of *The Man of Mode* are those of its period: by revealing the shape of those conflicts accurately, Etherege's play attains truthfulness to human experience.

However, it is the moral issue which has dominated (and obfuscated) discussion ever since the argument between Steele and John Dennis in 1722. Dorimant's character is the crux, as a brief summary of his role shows. The rake-hero is introduced in his dressing-room preparing for action in his chosen arena—the Mall and London's private houses. Surrounded by tradespeople, his friends, and his servant, he reveals how he plans to cast off one mistress, Mrs Loveit, in favour of her closest friend Bellinda, who though sophisticated and worldly enough, had yet to have an affair. Moreover, he intends, with Bellinda's active help, to trick Mrs Loveit into rejecting him. In the course of Act I he learns of the arrival in London of a beautiful young heiress, and at the end of the Act he is shown sending money to a town whore. Despite some near-setbacks, Dorimant does succeed in seducing Bellinda, does cast off Mrs Loveit, and ends the comedy having certainly won Hariet's heart, and almost certainly her hand, without entirely foreclosing the possibility of continued relationships with both Bellinda and Mrs Loveit. The bare bones of the plot show Dorimant's kinship with Don Juan, another seventeenth-century creation who stands as a naturalist and rationalist antagonist to the *précieux* idealizing of Courtly Love. (Just as Machiavelli's semimythic status reflects the emotional and intellectual crisis consequent upon the discovery of *Realpolitik* in the late sixteenth and seventeenth centuries, and Faustus testifies to the scientific assault on the boundaries of God-given knowledge, so Don Juan is a response to a related crisis in sexual attitudes.) Not surprisingly the play's imagery persistently aligns Dorimant with the Devil—for Lady Woodvill he is 'prince of all the devils in the town' (III.iii, 105–6).[30] But if Dorimant is allied to Don Juan and hence to the libertine and sceptical strain in seventeenth-century culture, whose most obvious contemporary exemplar was Etherege's fellow-wit, Lord Rochester, *The Man of Mode* is not an exploration of the myth's most radical consequences. Unlike Mozart's heroically fated figure he does not face the Commendatore and end in Hell; nor does Etherege's comedy allow Dorimant's delight in controlling others to become the utter ruthlessness of the Vicomte de Valmont and Marquise de Merteuil in *Les Liaisons dangereuses* (1782). Dorimant inhabits a youthful and less extreme world which is predominantly comic in tone, and which, moreover,

[30] See too I, 100, II.ii, 15, V.ii, 218.

superimposes the Rake Reformed pattern onto that of the libertine trickster.

It is the combination of the two patterns which upsets the moralists. Is the scheming intriguer who attains true love and the favours of his mistresses no more than a promiscuous cynic endorsed by the play? Is the gaiety merely heartless? Jeremy Collier is the first in the long line of critics who have thought so. His complaint was that Restoration comedy presented 'Vice under Characters of advantage'. In his reading, 'A finish'd Libertine seldom fails of making his fortune upon the *Stage* . . . there is great Care taken to furnish him with Breeding and Address: He is presently put into a Post of Honour, and an Equipage of Sense: and if he does the worst, he is pretty sure of speaking the best Things; I mean the most lively and entertaining'.[31] Drama ought not to reward sexual misdoing with marriage to the heroine. But it is the claims to gentility, to being a pattern of 'politeness' (that is, of gentlemanly conduct), which really sticks in the throat of the moralist. Dean Lockier exactly caught the paradox which most incensed the play's critics when he called Dorimant a 'genteel rake of wit'.[32] To the accusation of sinfulness is added that of social snobbery. Not only does Dorimant belong to a stylish (and idle) middle class, but, with the play's endorsement, he takes for granted the superiority of sophisticated stylishness to the dull morality of the Dissenting clergyman.

All of this is there: it is not the facts that are at issue but the attitude the audience should take to Dorimant. The crucial question is in what way does (or should) the audience identify with Dorimant? A direct moral questioning of the comedy in Collier's manner is fundamentally wrongheaded because it does not recognize the particular way in which comedy is serious. The same is in the end true of Dale Underwood's very good book *Etherege and the Seventeenth Century Comedy of Manners*. Underwood's sympathetic and scholarly investigation of the Libertine, Hobbesian, and Epicurean attitudes which lie behind the play gives essential background from the history of ideas for an understanding of the play, but in his hands *The Man of Mode* is less a play than an expression of a philosophical argument. The effect of Underwood's scholarship is to leave us where we began, with a singularly unpleasant human being on our hands.

What is necessary is to take the play out of the study and onto the stage, and to ask about the audience's reaction. Harriet Hawkins rightly points out that any critical response must take account of

---

[31] *Dissuasive from the Play-House* (1703), p. 4.
[32] Joseph Spence, *Anecdotes*, ed. cit., No. 678 (1–6 September 1730).

the fact that 'audiences have often delighted in characters ... who have the pride, energy, intelligence, cunning, or power to overleap moral fences and to invert traditional values'.[33] The dramatist pleases his audience, and it is the critic who perceives the moral headaches (and who must, to quote Beckett, provide his own aspirins). After making this point, Professor Hawkins goes on, I think, to betray her own insight. Finding that the 'righteous solemnity' of critics like Jocelyn Powell and Underwood distorts the comic emphasis of Etherege's play, she sees the comedy as much gayer, and much less serious:

> The games people play in Etherege's comedy are timeless (if trivial) ones, and like [Ovid's] *Art of Love*, *The Man of Mode* is still amusing and relevant enough on its own terms ... For the light comic spirit pervading the play allows us to look at the social spectacles that it mirrors and magnifies and see them as—spectacles. The primary purpose of this comedy seems to be neither immoral nor moral, but rather spectacular ... a glittering, amusing, and witty dramatic spectacle.[34]

This passage seems guilty of some confusion. Comedy, like all art, resembles a game in that it causes nothing to happen: it is for free. It differs from the social games played in everyday life, which are real—if they are merely 'trivial', then so much the worse for our relationships with others. But if in one sense the audience is uninvolved because watching a 'spectacle', it is also, in a way not easily attained in real life, involved. Since we watch for free, we are also free to see ourselves (or other possible selves freed from the restrictions adopted by or imposed upon the individual) in the characters and actions displayed on the stage. The realistic texture of Restoration comedy makes it easy to overlook the way in which all drama triggers a psychodrama within the individual members of the audience—indeed, within the audience as a whole: the audience in a public theatre can rarely be so homogeneous as to ignore the divisions within its own society, and it is clear that the response to *The Man of Mode* on the part of the servants and tradespeople in the upper gallery differed from that of the middle-class woman in the boxes, and that both differed from the reaction of those in the pit. An audience is dynamically implicated in what happens on the stage. It cannot merely watch, but must judge and choose between the characters and their deeds. Further, it is the dramatist who provides the frame of reference: if the audience chooses to see the play (that is, does not walk out), then it must discriminate between the characters depicted and, at one level, within standards set up by

---

[33] *Likenesses of Truth in Elizabethan and Restoration Comedy* (Oxford, 1972), p. 81.
[34] ibid., pp. 93–4.

the play's dominant concepts. In *The Man of Mode* there is no doubt that Dorimant would at least be stimulating, while Sir Fopling would quickly become tedious.

Comedy deals with topics close to its audience, and is aggressive and violent towards its butts to an extent not usually permissible in society. It is correspondingly over-generous to its victors. Its characteristic targets are anxieties or constrictions which the audience normally accepts out of necessity without altogether liking them. One function of comedy (and humour) is undoubtedly to release aggression and anxiety, especially the anxiety and aggression surrounding sexuality, which provides its own forms of embarrassment and unease for each successive generation. The rake hero gains the audience's support because he acts out that side of his audience's psyche which is in real life either denied, or compromised, by the ties or obligations of society. Since comedy in this form often combines the appearance of subversiveness while actually supporting more conservative values (Dorimant is after all bound for marriage with Harriet), it could be reduced to a sociological function—a safe release for feelings otherwise dangerous to society's stability. Aristotle's belief that comedy originated from the ancient Greek phallic songs, and the Roman institution of Saturnalia, indicate that the genre's roots lie in deliberate inversion of social values and hierarchies for a set time-limit, and in the vitality and disruptiveness of human sexuality.

A truer, and less anthropologically reductive, account of comedy needs to insist that its confusions and inversions reflect the audience's knowledge that life itself does not fit obediently into any moral patterns. Even a set of strongly held and coherent moral beliefs cannot ensure proper behaviour, especially within personal relationships, a main subject of this play. Though people need to act up to their beliefs, they are only too likely to fail to do so. There is even an inherent ridiculousness in the continued pursuit of what must be betrayed by experience, yet too open an admission of that truth would incapacitate the individual from action, or lead swiftly to cynicism.

The moral issue inevitably focuses attention on Dorimant. Yet the case for *The Man of Mode* must be drawn from the whole play: it is the contrast with other attitudes and characters, along with the interplay between themes, which defines Dorimant's vitality and ambiguity. And the play as a whole reflects the strains and tensions of a society in a state of flux over attitudes to gentility, marriage, and sexual behaviour. Judging from the varying responses to Dorimant within the comedy, he is as ambiguous within the play as for later critics. The most obvious conflict is that between generations. Lady Woodvill, an 'antiquated beauty' and 'a great admirer of the forms and civility of the last age', still hankers after the *précieux* modes of courtesy of the Court of Charles I and Henrietta Maria. In her view Dorimant 'delights in nothing but in rapes and riots' (III.iii, 106). She has, of course, seriously misjudged Dorimant. His style is not carousing and whoring, but the four bullies who insult Bellinda and Mrs Loveit in III.iii show that this kind of violently aggressive anti-feminist manhood was still to be found in London—though the play would like to suggest that its practitioners were now drawn from inferior levels of society with City rather than Court connections. Manners have changed: Dorimant, despite his Danish serenade of Mrs Loveit (II.i, 116), belongs to a far more dangerous category—the genteel rake, who pursues his women not in whorehouses but in private houses (III.ii, 95–6). Placing gentlewomen at risk adds both a new seriousness and a new danger to the game. Both the wits and the representatives of conservative values, Lady Woodvill and Old Bellair, agree that there has been a significant change in manners. What the wits enjoy, and their 'gravities' (III.i, 110) resent, are the 'freedoms of the present' (I, 113). The most obvious freedom is the practice of keeping a mistress: Dorimant claims that even judges have set an example in countenancing this, 'the crying sin o' the nation' (I, 141–2), though Lady Woodvill's naivety prevents her from perceiving the true cause of a judge's attentions to her own daughter, Harriet (I, 135–41). It is an age in which a pretty face and discreet promiscuity will help a woman climb the social ladder—'she may come to keep her coach and pay parish duties, if the good humour of the age continues', and so become, in Medley's words, one 'of the number of the ladies kept by public-spirited men for the good of the whole town' (IV.ii, 73–6). And *The Man of Mode*, no doubt with licence, suggests that the practice was common to all classes of fashionable town life.

Unsurprisingly then, Lady Woodvill asserts 'Lewdness is the business now; love was the business in my time' (IV.i, 14). The kind of love she has in mind is that of protesting lovers, suffering the flames of unrequited love on behalf of an unyielding mistress, a mode recorded ironically enough in Waller's poetry, so often quoted by Dorimant. Courtly love is only possible within a hierarchical society, and Lady Woodvill despairs of the confusions of rank in contemporary society. Playing the character of Mr Courtage, a man made of the 'forms and commonplaces, sucked out of the remaining lees of the last age', Dorimant agrees: 'Forms and ceremonies, the only things that uphold quality and greatness, are now shamefully laid aside and neglected'. Social barriers are crumbling—'All people mingle nowadays' (IV.i, 8). When Old Bellair censures the modern gallants for their disrespect, Lady

Woodvill bursts out, 'Quality was then considered, and not rallied by every fleering fellow ... 'Tis good breeding now to be civil to none but players and Exchange women. They are treated by 'em as much above their condition as others are below theirs' (III.i, 119–24).

As a Royalist and conservative, Lord Clarendon in his analysis of post-Civil War England shares Lady Woodvill's concern,[35] and Act I of *The Man of Mode* bears out the sense of social confusion from the beginning. Dorimant's easy bantering with Foggy Nan and the Shoemaker may depend upon Dorimant's assumptions of superior-ity, but it plainly indicates an undue familiarity with tradesmen and Exchange women, based on mutual interests—Dorimant's ability to pay and, on both sides, a love of the game. Not only are social distinctions sapped from within by the failure of the gentleman-rake to behave decorously towards inferiors, but the urban working class is corrupted by the wits' life style. According to the Shoemaker, apprentices have abandoned their 'harmless' traditional ballads in favour of the wits' scurrilous 'damned lampoons' (I, 243). The Shoemaker himself has attained a dubious sophistication in his marriage—"Zbud, there's never a man i' the town lives more like a gentleman with his wife than I do. I never mind her motions; she never inquires into mine. We speak to one another civilly, hate one another heartily, and because 'tis vulgar to lie and soak together, we have each of us our several settle-bed' (I, 265–9).

The corruption of the lower orders through the imitation of their social betters, and the aspirations to gentility on the part of the servants of the fashionable, are as marked in Etherege's London as Fielding's. Although seen a good deal more benignly, *The Man of Mode* reflects the extent that city life and its attendant anonymity led to freedom and a rejection of accepted roles and values. Foggy Nan recognizes the Shoemaker as an enemy: although she does not mind what gentlemen say, she despises him as a 'foul-mouthed rogue' and a 'dirty fellow' precisely because he apes the modish libertine values of Dorimant. He is a 'heathen' and an 'atheist'. Medley chides him—'You have brought the envy of the world upon you by living above yourself. Whoring and swearing are vices too genteel for a shoemaker' (I, 234–6). But in this upside-down world, the Shoemaker gives as good as he gets: "Zbud, I think you men of quality will grow as unreasonable as the women: you would engross the sins o' the nation. Poor folks can no sooner be wicked

---

[35] See *The Continuation of the Life of Edward, Earl of Clarendon* printed with *The Life* (1759), vol. 2, 21–2. Cited by Christopher Hill, *Puritanism and Revolution* (1958), which provides valuable background to the period (see especially chapters 6, 9, and 14).

but they're railed at by their betters' (I, 237–9). The whole concept of gentility is called into question (and the large number of courtesy books published in these years indicates that concern was not restricted to the comedies).[36]

The ambiguities of Dorimant's London cannot, however, be resolved by any appeal to established values. Lady Woodvill's outmoded ideas of gallantry and subordination give no viable alternative. They cannot because they ignore the facts of society and because, in the persons of Lady Woodvill and Old Bellair, they are inconsistent and hypocritical. The real grounds for Lady Woodvill's hatred of the 'depraved appetite of this vicious age' are that her beauty is no longer admired: the younger generation 'tastes nothing but green fruit and loathes it when 'tis kindly ripened' (IV.i, 40–1). 'Kindly', which can also mean fully ripened according to its nature, is a witty reminder of the vitality of the natural forces which manners seek to control, and which Lady Woodvill denies. A similarly muddled and self-congratulatory note is evident in Lady Woodvill's companion in foolish age, Old Bellair. He objects to 'idle town flirts' because they do not bring the 'blessing of a good estate' (II.i, 60): indeed, the young people have gone so far as to get 'an ill habit of preferring beauty, no matter where they find it' (III.i, 125–6). For them marriage is a mercenary and social affair: sons and daughters should be governed by their parents. Indeed, Lady Woodvill's coeval is deeply antipathetic to women as anything but sex objects. The conclusion of the *bachique* in which he joins is indicative of his sexual ethos—'Wine and beauty by turns great souls should inspire; /Present all together—and now, boys, give fire!' (IV.i, 382–3). There is no room for mutual feeling in his idea of courtship. Harriet protests when Old Bellair urges her proposed match with Young Bellair, 'You expect we should fall to and love as gamecocks fight, as soon as we are set together. Adod, you're unreasonable!' (III.i, 167–9). Old Bellair's comic attempts at courting the young and attractive Emilia are coarse and anti-verbal. When asked to praise Emilia's dancing he can only say the opposite of what he means—'... go, bid her dance no more. It don't become her, it don't become her. Tell her I say so. (*Aside*) Adod, I love her' (IV.i, 5–7). His boorishness, his assumption of total authority over his son, and his pursuit of financial advantage over personal happiness where his son's marriage is concerned,

[36] For instance, *The Art of Making Love: or, Rules for the Conduct of Ladies and Gallants in their Amours.* ... (1676) by 'S. C.', which is largely taken from the French of Boulanger, and *Art of Complaisance or the Means to oblige in Conversation.* ... (1673), which W. L. Ustick notes is in the main translated from De Refuge's *Traité de la Cour* (?1618), *Review of English Studies*, vol. 5 (1929), 149–53. See also II.i, 124, 128 and notes.

give the lie to any claims his generation can make for superiority: both he and Lady Woodvill are 'unreasonable'. Lady Woodvill's assertion, 'Well, this is not the women's age, let 'em think what they will' (IV.i, 13) is exactly wrong. The new freedoms may bring more danger, but they also offer more choice and the chance of self-determination. As P. F. Vernon has argued, the comedy of Wycherley and Etherege is not hostile to the institution of marriage itself, but it is opposed to marriages of convenience. He aptly cites H. J. Habakkuk's work on patterns of marriage in the period to demonstrate that following the Interregnum and its sequestrations, alliances for dynastic and financial reasons posed a serious problem in the upper classes.[37] Wycherley's concern is evident from the title of one of his poems, 'An Heroic Epistle, To the Most Honourable Match-Maker, a Bawd, call'd J.C.—; proving Free Love more Honourable, than Slavish, Mercenary Marriage'. The younger generation in *The Man of Mode* is in revolt against the repressions of an older generation, and feels itself to have achieved an important degree of freedom.

Lady Woodvill and Old Bellair represent an extreme response to Dorimant, one which is to be upended by the play's conclusion: Lady Townley, whose role is that of a worldly-wise member of the elder generation, tolerant and in sympathy with the young, rightly forecasts that Lady Woodvill will 'find Mr Dorimant as civil a gentleman as you thought Mr Courtage' (V.ii, 283–4). But the reaction to Dorimant amongst his immediate associates is equally confused. Sir Fopling regards him an English exemplar of French gallantry, but grievously mistakes the purpose of gallantry in Dorimant's world—'women', says Sir Fopling, 'are the prettiest things we can fool away our time with' (IV.i, 220–1). For Medley he is a mentor in dissembling, cunning, and malice; for servants and tradespeople he is a generous man of the world who refuses to stand on ceremony; Mrs Loveit's responses range from violent rejection of him as a 'prodigy of ill nature' and a barbarian, to an unwilling admiration—'I know he is a devil, but he has something of the angel yet undefaced in him, which makes him so charming and agreeable that I must love him, be he never so wicked' (II.ii, 15–17). If Bellinda is forced to recognize his 'ill nature' (II.ii, 256), Dorimant himself ironically lays claim to good nature (I, 5), while Emilia thinks that the 'town does him a great deal of injury', and that he is 'very witty' (III.ii, 22, 27). In Lady Townley's eyes he is

[37] Marriage of Convenience and the Moral Code of Restoration Comedy', *Essays in Criticism*, vol. 12 (1962), 370–87. He refers to Habakkuk's 'Marriage Settlements in the Eighteenth Century', *Transactions of the Royal Historical Society*, 4th series, vol. 32 (1950), 15–32, and 'English Landownership, 1680–1740', *Economic History Review*, vol. 10 (1940), 2–17.

'a very well-bred man' and a 'very pleasant acquaintance' (ibid., 25, 35–6). Young Bellair believes Dorimant to have 'something extreme delightful in his wit and person' and, above all, to be 'so easy and so natural', an ease and naturalness which Harriet castigates as affectation—'He's agreeable and pleasant, I must own, but he does so much affect being so, he displeases me . . . It passes on the easy town, who are favourably pleased in him to call it humour' (III.iii, 18–27). The protean nature of Dorimant is a natural consequence of his role as trickster, though it equally reflects on many of the play's characters' inability to distinguish between appearance and reality in the world of manners, and to grasp the questioning relationship in which he stands to 'true love'.

Young Bellair and Emilia are true love's representatives in *The Man of Mode*, and are what passes in this play for the *ingénu* lovers. They are very carefully set apart from the young rakes about town. Dorimant defines Young Bellair as a 'handsome, well-bred, and by much the most tolerable of all the young men that do not abound in wit' (I, 371–2). Emilia is also described negatively by Medley—

> Emilia, give her her due, has the best reputation of any young woman about the town who has beauty enough to provoke detraction. Her carriage is unaffected, her discourse modest—not at all censorious nor pretending, like the counterfeits of the age. (I, 383–7).

The positive and vital quality of 'wit' then, which is allied to 'malice', belongs to Dorimant and Medley, 'men of sense, who will be talking reason' (I, 282), men who argue, that is, the irrationality of marriage when the irregular demands of sexuality are more easily and satisfactorily met outside the narrow obligations of a legal tie. 'Is it not', Medley asks of Young Bellair, who is firmly committed to marrying Emilia, 'great indiscretion for a man of credit, who may have money enough on his word, to go and deal with Jews, who for little sums make men enter into bonds and give judgments [i.e., securities]?' (I, 298–300). As 'wits' Medley and Dorimant embody what the word had come to mean in colloquial language. Richard Flecknoe, in a work published in 1675 and probably alluded to satirically by Medley as belonging to the last age, observes, '*wit* now [is] but new names for an *Atheist* and *Debauchée*'.[38] The alliance between the wits and libertine strains of thought was one felt by contemporaries, and given countenance by the circulation of Rochester's libertine lyrics in the 1670s even had they not been backed up by his well-known escapades.

From this viewpoint, Young Bellair's love for Emilia denies him the 'heaven' of promiscuity in return for the 'hell' of marriage.

<hr />

[38] *A Treatise of the Sports of Wit* (1675), p. 5, the work probably alluded to by Medley at II.i, 124.

Although *The Man of Mode* respects the relationship of Emilia and Young Bellair, they are seen as less perceptive and less vital than Harriet or Dorimant. Their idealism as romantic lovers necessarily limits them. Emilia's distaste for fools is regarded by Lady Townley as 'a little too delicate' (III.ii, 119), exhibiting a lack of the robust tolerance of the older woman. ''Tis good to have an universal taste. We should love wit, but for variety be able to divert ourselves with the extravagancies of those who want it' (ibid., 113–15). (An attitude endorsed by the audience to the extent that it finds Sir Fopling's idiocies laughable.) Yet in this comedy Emilia is as sharply aware of the unsurety of the human heart as the wits —'Do not vow—our love is frail as is our life, and full as little in our power; and are you sure you shall outlive this day?' (II.i, 26–7). Even the romantic lovers must take account of a realism based on 'reasonable' arguments. Love is again and again described in images which demystify its claims to absoluteness by presenting it in naturalistic and materialistic terms—as a sickness, a legal battle, a pleasurable 'business', a kind of hunting, a card-game, a battle, and so on. Love is essentially irrational and temporary in its nature, a fact recognized by both the characters and the audience. Men, in a society which countenances it, are only too likely to give rein to their appetites (women too, though they have to guard against their reputations being affected). Harriet, speaking of Dorimant, remarks on the 'sordidness of men's natures' (III.iii, 68). It is an unflattering assumption, but is nevertheless one kind of observable truth about human behaviour. These attitudes and the assumption of impermanence leave very little reasonable space for 'true love'.

Yet *The Man of Mode* does finally allow the two different pairs of young lovers to come together. Young Bellair and Emilia employ a benign and easily accomplished trick marriage in order to fool their parents, but Dorimant and Harriet have to approach one another much more warily through the rites of a witty courtship and other dangers.

The particular formulation of *The Man of Mode*'s balance between apparent cynicism, comic tolerance, and emotional honesty, depends importantly upon the interplay between key words, which embody a complex of tensions in contemporary anxieties about love and manners. From the first act, Dorimant and Harriet are linked by their shared 'wildness', which distinguishes them from all other characters in the play. Dorimant is one of 'the wild young men o' the town' (I, 100): Harriet has more wit 'than is usual in her sex, and as much malice. Then, she's as wild as you would wish her, and has a demureness in her looks that makes it so surprising' (I, 129–31). The combination of wit, wildness, and the ability to dissemble are shared by both future lovers, and it is their wildness, and malice which separate them from Young Bellair and Emilia. In Dorimant's eyes Harriet is above all 'wild, witty, love-some, beautiful, and young' (III.iii, 312–13). The word's frequent occurrences in the play call on a wide range of meanings. It can mean merely 'restive', as when Harriet threatens to shake her hair out of order (III.i, 3), but the word's connotations extend to the ideas of gaiety, of fecklessness, of resisting control, even of ferocity and savagery. Harriet makes its links with her sexual attractiveness apparent when she says, 'My eyes are wild and wandering like my passions, and cannot yet be tied to rules of charming' (IV.i, 105–6). Dorimant, of course, is often described as 'wild' (I, 100, IV.i, 64–5, 301), and Harriet calls him 'ridiculously wild and apish' (V.ii, 56), mockingly though significantly relating him to the animal world. This clustering of meanings suggests that when Bellinda calls him a 'wild man' (II.ii, 93), we are to remember the 'wild man' of legend.[39] The figure of the wild man, sexually and morally unconstrained by society's restrictions, clearly echoes Libertine aspirations, and Maximillian Novak has pointed out that the word has a particular resonance in the comedy of the 1670s.[40] The hero's and heroine's wildness in *The Man of Mode* is dangerous for others and, potentially, for the lovers. Both choose to live at risk, Dorimant obviously so, but Harriet's preference of the 'scandalous Mall' (III.iii, 272), with its assignations and dangerous 'conversations', to the more formal but reputable Hyde Park, is telling—'... I abominate the dull diversions there [Hyde Park]—the formal bows, the affected smiles, the silly by-words and amorous tweers in passing. Here one meets with a little conversation now and then' (III.iii, 35–8). Style and good conversation go together, and it is to the point that Pall Mall was close to St James's and actually built at Charles II's instructions.

Harriet's 'wildness' is integral to her sexual attractiveness, and Medley's connoisseur's description lingers over her 'lively, large, wanton eyes' (I, 120–1). Although able to remain within the bounds of propriety through her charm and manipulation of those

[39] Maximillian Novak makes the same connection in 'Margery Pinchwife's "London Disease": Restoration Comedy and the Libertine Offensive of the 1670's', *Studies in the Literary Imagination*, vol. 10 (1977), 16. For a brief account, with helpful references, of the history of the 'wild man', see *The Tempest*, ed. Frank Kermode (5th ed., 1954), pp. xxxviii–ix and note.

[40] Novak, op. cit., pp. 1–24, who points out that the heroines of Shadwell's *Epsom-Wells* (1672) worry that Bevil and Rains are 'so very wild', while 'wildness' is associated with Libertine values throughout Wycherley's *Country Wife* (acted 1675).

about her, Harriet is essentially untamed, and her sometimes freakish and 'extravagant' behaviour (III.i, 28, III.iii, 6) is an accepted part of her character.[41] 'Extravagance' and wildness are also joined in the character of Dorimant. With sharp dramatic irony Lady Woodvill defines 'a wild, extravagant fellow of the times' as 'a Dorimant' when she believes herself to be talking to Mr Courtage (IV.i, 301).

It has recently been suggested that the idea of extravagance is a defining quality of several rake-heroes in Restoration comedy:

> Wycherley's Horner (an extravagant trickster), Etherege's Dorimant (an extravagant narcissist) and Congreve's Valentine, who assumes madness for much of *Love for Love*, are all extravagants. In making the extravagant city rake into a comic protagonist, the playwrights gave him something equivalent to the qualities that were supposed to arouse 'admiration' in the rhymed heroic plays of this decade, including a degree of excess in word and character.[42]

In *The Man of Mode*, however, extravagance seems to be regarded as one element of the wild and witty hero and heroine, for extravagance is a dubious quality. Mrs Loveit's 'mighty spirit' prevents her from keeping a balance between a passionate nature and the need for self-control: 'She's the most passionate in her love and the most extravagant in her jealousy of any woman I ever heard of' (I, 162–3). The extravagance of uncontrolled passion creates a fatal vulnerability—Dorimant even throws in her face the 'extravagancies' to which he claims to have been driven by his passion for her (V.i, 180). As Medley says, love and jealousy rage strangely in her, and her attraction to Dorimant meets the needs of a self-destructive element in her character—'She could not have picked out a devil upon earth so proper to torment her' (II.i, 111–12). The psychological accuracy of Etherege's portrait of Mrs Loveit is important: she too is driven by arrogance and a love for power, and is therefore doomed to choose a man like Dorimant. Mrs Loveit is the creature of her own excesses and, consequently, the butt of the comedy's most savage ridicule. She shows a foolish disregard for the realities of life when she tells Pert that she 'had rather be made infamous [by Dorimant's malicious gossip] than owe my reputation to the dull discretion of those fops you talk of' (II.ii, 46–7). Even when she nearly has Dorimant in retreat (after raising his jealousy by pretending to be really attracted by Sir Fopling), her feelings cause her to throw away her advantage (V.i, 200–1). Her outcries against Dorimant are marked by their hysterical rhetoric: 'Plague,

---

[41] See Robert Jordan, 'The Extravagant Rake in Restoration Comedy', *Restoration Literature*, ed. Harold Love (1972), pp. 69–88.
[42] Novak, art. cit., p. 16, who modifies Jordan's findings.

war, famine, fire—all that can bring universal ruin and misery on mankind—with joy I'd perish to have you in my power but this moment!' (II.ii, 250-3). Her last extravagance, before she abandons the stage, is to advise Bellinda to give herself up to goodness (V.ii, 338-9).

If the world of the play punishes Mrs Loveit savagely—Dorimant's assessment of her future is coldly clinical (V.i, 136-9), and Harriet is brutally tart ('Mr Dorimant has been your God Almighty long enough. 'Tis time to think of another' (V.ii, 340-1))—it is because Mrs Loveit, unlike Sir Fopling, knows the penalties but chooses to ignore them. Passion reduces her to the level of a comic automaton. The sternness of her rejection stems from her demonstration of the destructiveness of love: she has believed what Dorimant calls the 'extravagant words' men speak in love. ' 'Tis as unreasonable to expect we should perform all we promise then, as do all we threaten when we are angry' (V.ii, 264-6). It is the extravagance of love's hopes in a materialistically reasonable world which makes both Dorimant and Harriet slow to admit their feelings for one another, and which means that they must engage in a carefully indirect courtship. *The Man of Mode* is unforgiving only towards Mrs Loveit. Her exclusion can be handled openly and schematically because comedy's conventions allow it to encompass comfortably what would be profoundly embarrassing in life. More radically, she cannot be forgiven because she represents the fate of Dorimant or Harriet if they lose their balance and control. This is not to deny that Dorimant's character is in some part compromised by his affair with Mrs Loveit, but from the comic standpoint Mrs Loveit gets what she deserves.

The other obvious extravagant in the play is Sir Fopling, who mistakes manner for substance. There is a marked undertow which hints that Dorimant may, in his own way, be as much a man of mode as the Frenchified knight. Harriet's accusations of affectation show her realization that Dorimant plays to his audience. And it is Mrs Loveit and Bellinda who recognize that Dorimant's pursuit of women is self-regarding, a pursuit of the town's admiration and not of anything more—'You take a pride of late in using of me ill, that the town may know the power you have over me ...' (V.i, 153-4). Vanity, then, may be a motive force behind Dorimant as much as it is for Sir Fopling, who is at least harmless. Dorimant's other main drive, the love of power, is even less morally attractive. He takes more pleasure in a woman's ruin than her love (V.i, 171-2), and, as Bellinda says, is 'never well but when he triumphs—nay, glories—to a woman's face in his villainies' (V.i, 248-9). The connection with Hobbes's definition of 'glory' has been made by Dale Underwood: 'Joy, arising from imagination of a man's own power and ability, is that exultation of the mind which is called GLORYING . . .'[43] The driving forces behind the sophistication of this modish society are those of domination and self-gratification. The vitalism of 'wildness' and 'extravagance' is offset by the dubious materialism which certainly informs the attitudes of Medley, and perhaps those of Lady Townley.

Within the social world depicted by *The Man of Mode*, the naked pursuit of these ends is contained and made tolerable by the Town's code of manners which places a high valuation on 'easiness' and 'complaisance'. Etherege's 'easy' character and style, that is one at once stylish and colloquial, impressed his contemporaries at once, and was still for Pope the mark of his achievement.[44] In *The Man of Mode* the word can be used of manners and behaviour, as when Young Bellair describes Dorimant to Harriet—'Lord, madam, all he does and says is so easy and so natural' (III.iii, 22). It can also apply to the grace and attractiveness of Harriet's figure, which Medley evokes as 'a fine, easy, clean shape' (I, 119), a phrase echoed by Dorimant (III.iii, 28). But when Harriet remarks upon the 'easy town', she comments both upon its tolerance and its gullibility.[45] The Town's tolerance is of only doubtful humanity, for it is marked by malice and a love of gossip. The double nature of society's good nature and ease is embodied in the multi-faceted idea of 'complaisance', a recent word drawn from the French, and one which focuses the aspirations and unease of a society reaching after a new form of *politesse*, in which appearance and true feeling might be widely at variance. One of the many conduct books published at the time is entitled *The Art of Complaisance or the Means to oblige in Conversation . . .* (1673).[46] Its motto, *Quis nescit dissimulare, nescit vivere* ('he who does not know how to dissimulate does not know how to live'), underscores the moral ambivalence which these works show towards the need to disguise feelings in order to succeed in social intercourse. Although they normally argue that such dissimulation is necessary and for the good of society, they shy away from the more cynical implications of such a division. The extent of the stress caused by this tension appears in the embarrassingly wide definition given by the author of *The Art of Complais-*

---

[43] *Leviathan, or The Matter, Forme, & Power of a Commonwealth, Ecclesiasticall and Civill* (1651), pp. 26–7.

[44] 'None of our writers have a freer, easier way for comedy than Etherege and Vanbrugh' (Joseph Spence, *Anecdotes*, ed. cit., No. 483).

[45] 'Easiness' again means gullibility as V.ii, 166; at IV.i, 146 it may carry the sense of unchastity.

[46] For an essay which interestingly relates this book and French works to the play, see John G. Hayman, 'Dorimant and the Comedy of A Man of Mode', *Studies in English Literature 1500–1900*, vol. 10 (1970), 459–68.

ance to his topic: 'I hope I may without provoking the too Critical, use this word Complaisance in such an extensive signification, as to comprehend reservation, dissimulation, dexterity, patience, humility, civility and affability ...' (p. 8). The same width of meaning is apparent in *The Man of Mode*. On several occasions it means no more than acting in such a way as to please others, as when Sir Fopling explains that his unwillingness to dance is not 'want of complaisance' (IV.i, 268; see too IV.i, 117 and V.i, 35). But when the word comes into Dorimant's orbit, the concept becomes much more slippery, for his wildness is accommodated within an effectively complaisant manner, which is a deliberate cover for his depredations. When Dorimant complains that women are as 'unreasonable' in their love affairs as at cards because unless they have won the game 'a man can never quietly give over when he's weary', Medley replies, 'If you would play without being obliged to complaisance, Dorimant, you should play in public places'. Taking his pursuit of women into 'private houses' means that Dorimant must endure social niceties (III.ii, 91–8). Consequently, he is under a necessity to create an image of politeness. His friendship with Young Bellair, 'always complaisant', is aimed at the town—

> It is our mutual interest to be so. It makes the women think the better of his understanding and judge more favourably of my reputation; it makes him pass upon some for a man of very good sense [i.e., as a witty rake], and I upon others for a very civil person. (I, 375–8)

Dorimant's appearance of civility is essential to his continued success. Hence the involutions of his rejection of Mrs Loveit: it is in the interest of both Dorimant and Bellinda that he should not appear to do a 'barbarous thing' (I, 199). The problem is that Dorimant's 'complaisance', while dangerous for its victims, is a valuable asset in Lady Townley's society (like Emilia, she finds him 'civil'). His civility is both feigned and real. Dorimant's case is the sharpest presentation of contemporary unease before the ambiguity inherent in the ideal of complaisance. It falls to Harriet to perceive his 'affectation', and to demand that if they are to marry, he must change.

Structurally, the play distinguishes between Dorimant's activities when he is heart-free and when courting Harriet. On the evidence of his relationships with Mrs Loveit and Bellinda, Dorimant is right to say, half-cynically, half-regretfully, that 'Love gilds us over and makes us show fine things to one another for a time, but soon the gold wears off, and then again the native brass appears' (II.ii, 185–7). But even in this world, he is not allowed to escape wholly untouched. In his relations with Mrs Loveit, whoever knows what is really in the other's heart can win the victory. As long as Dorimant knows that Loveit is jealous of him, he can manipulate her to his ends. The turning-point comes when he thinks she might really be interested in Sir Fopling. Admittedly, the cause is less passion for Loveit than concern for his reputation, but when he first mentions his fears in an aside, Dorimant significantly blames it on the irrationality of the heart:

MEDLEY

> ... I have known men fall into dangerous relapses when they have found a woman inclining to another.

DORIMANT *(to himself)*

> He guesses the secret of my heart. I am concerned but dare not show it, lest Bellinda should mistrust all I have done to gain her.

(III.iii, 265–8)

His anger almost leads to the disruption of his carefully ordered life. When Bellinda finds him at Mrs Loveit's in Act V, Scene i he has to bear with the two women berating him, and to admit, 'I am to blame in some circumstances, I confess . . .' (ll. 261–2). Even then, he is not entirely free of the danger, for when both his mistresses appear in the final scene, he is taken aback—'Loveit and Bellinda! The devil owes me a shame today, and I think never will have done paying it' (V.ii, 218–19). Although Dorimant recovers balance, and these temporary setbacks can hardly be rated as punishment, it is clear that his ascendancy depends wholly upon his wit controlling his passions.

Dorimant's real defeat is at Harriet's hands. The play almost goes out of its way to assure the audience that it is a case of love at first sight for them both. On Dorimant's first glimpse of Harriet he thinks of marriage; 'I'll follow the lottery and put in for a prize with my friend Bellair' (III.iii, 30–1), and left in a 'reverie' after his first conversation with her, he quotes from Waller's 'Of Loving at First Sight':

> Snatched from myself, how far behind
> Already I behold the shore!

Simultaneously, Dorimant is sharply aware of the danger this represents: '. . . she has left a pleasing image of herself behind that wanders in my soul. —It must not settle there' (ibid., 114–15). Dorimant fears the ultimate irrationality of love, and recognizes the danger of the loss of his own sense of identity (just as Mrs Loveit has) in a world in which, since everyone pursues 'glory', a coherent identity is extremely hard to maintain: 'I love her and dare not let her know it. I fear she has an ascendant o'er me and may revenge the wrongs I have done her sex' (IV.i, 132–3). Equally, Harriet is overwhelmed by her attraction to Dorimant.

Even when she has only seen him at a distance, she is inclined towards him (III.i, 51, 90), and at her first meeting has to hide her feelings—'I feel as great a change within, but he shall never know it' (III.iii, 56). Other observers in the play, such as Busy, Medley, and Young Bellair, are sure of her feelings towards Dorimant (IV.ii, 157, V.ii, 49, 52). Harriet is at root a romantic heroine, opposed to the mercenary values of her mother's generation: 'Shall I be paid down by a covetous parent for a purchase? I need no land. No, I'll lay myself out all in love. It is decreed' (III.i, 63–4). But she is realistic enough to recognize Dorimant's fear of committing himself to love, and shrewd enough to know that she must not only prove his equal but establish a superiority in their courtship. Their mutual ability as actors sets them apart from the other characters. Dorimant acts the part of Mr Courtage (IV.i) and mimics Sir Fopling (V.i, 78 ff): Harriet acts out the role of young lover with Young Bellair to fool their parents (III.i), and mimics Dorimant (I, 58–9; III.iii, 82–92; IV.i, 95–8). Both accuse each other of acting for their respective audiences in the Mall (III.iii, 83–92). Their adroitness allows each to approach the other warily, to explore the reality of their own and their prospective partner's feelings. In their exchange in Act IV, Scene i, Harriet establishes her ascendancy by forcing Dorimant to come to the point of professing his love, only to mock the foolish appearance of a lover's protestations. At his refusal to continue, Harriet makes it clear that she needs to test his love—'When your love's grown strong enough to make you bear being laughed at, I'll give you leave to trouble me with it' (155–6). Although very unlike *Love's Labour's Lost* in mood or emphasis, the parallel between Harriet's treatment of Dorimant and Rosalind's punishment of Berowne's excessive wit, and her imposition of a time before she will reward his suit, brings out the conventional and idealistic comic pattern common to both plays. Both plays too are concerned with the falsity and inflation of love's rhetoric. When Dorimant, adopting the language of the *précieux* lover 'in prospect of such a heaven', renounces wine and women, Harriet cuts through—'Hold! Though I wish you devout, I would not have you turn fanatic' (V.ii, 133–4). Where Shakespeare's comedy belongs to a romance world, the Town in Etherege's play is inimical to love, hence the poignancy of those moments in which, against all odds, and against elements in Dorimant's character, the two lovers recognize their feelings for one another. Behind the affectations and verbal games, what Harriet recognizes is a vitality and aliveness in Dorimant that matches her own. She also sees the need for Dorimant to change, and for her to allow him time. The comedy sees that mere manners degenerates into emptiness (Sir Fopling) or incapacitates the man from action (Medley is no more than an observer). The wildness of Harriet and Dorimant lies ultimately in their willingness to risk themselves, while they, like the audience, know the risks involved.

The final scene brings together the various strands of the comedy, but allows the audience no easy resting place. Harriet's recognition of Dorimant's love is expressed in a new rhetoric of love which is at once knowing and idealistic. In the following exchange Harriet's reminders of Dorimant's past would be acerbic if it were not understood by both that behind the parleying lies real feeling, that real 'generosity' is involved on both sides—

EMILIA
    ... Here are dreadful preparations, Mr Dorimant—writings sealing, and a parson sent for.
DORIMANT
    To marry this lady?
BUSY
    Condemned she is; and what will become of her I know not, without you generously engage in a rescue.
DORIMANT
    In this sad condition, madam, I can do no less than offer you my service.
HARRIET
    The obligation is not great; you are the common sanctuary for all young women who run from their relations.
DORIMANT
    I have always my arms open to receive the distressed. But I will open my heart and receive you where none yet did ever enter. You have filled it with a secret, might I but let you know it—
HARRIET
    Do not speak it if you would have me believe it. Your tongue is so famed for falsehood, 'twill do the truth an injury.   *Turns away her head*
                                                                                (V.ii, 103–16)

The real conversation here is unspoken. In the lovers' hands the cynical patterns of witty town conversation have become the vehicle for expressing the sentiments of Waller, who is quoted by both, but whose language and vocabulary are no longer viable.[47] The comedy moves in its conclusion towards re-establishing the norms of generosity, good nature, and mutual love, so discovering a new stylishness through which to affirm conservative values.

What distinguishes *The Man of Mode* from the Shakespearean world is the way in which this moment of affirmation is not allowed to conclude the play's movement. Instead, *The Man of Mode* turns back to the problem of Mrs Loveit and Bellinda, and Dorimant faces both women with Harriet. His just-discovered faith in love does not prevent him from presenting his forthcoming marriage as

[47] See Ronald Berman, 'The Comic Passions of *The Man of Mode*', *Studies in English Literature 1500–1900*, vol. 10 (1970), 459–68.

purely materialistic in its motive—'Believe me—a wife, to repair the ruins of my estate that needs it' (V.ii, 258). The placing of this scene after the encounter between Harriet and Dorimant does mean that it hangs threateningly over their future relationship: it is significant that although Harriet knows that Mrs Loveit has been Dorimant's mistress, she does not know of his affair with Bellinda. The play, like most good jokes, looks in two directions. The comic pattern imposes the wish for a happy ending, yet the play has shown all too clearly the enemies to that happiness within the characters and within their society. Nevertheless, the ideal remains a possible if difficult one, and it is this balance between the possible and the probable that gives the poignancy to Dorimant and Harriet's final exchange, an exchange which turns on the opposition between Town and Country underlying the whole play. An essential condition placed by Harriet upon Dorimant is that he should prove his love by visiting her in the country:[48]

> To a great, rambling, lone house that looks as it were not inhabited, the family's so small. There you'll find my mother, an old lame aunt, and myself, sir, perched up on chairs at a distance in a large parlour, sitting moping like three or four melancholy birds in a spacious volary. Does not this stagger your resolution?

DORIMANT
> Not at all, madam. The first time I saw you, you left me with the pangs of love upon me, and this day my soul has quite given up her liberty.
>
> (V.ii, 368–75)

In obeying the Rake Reformed pattern *The Man of Mode* does not simply fall back upon conventional values. Dorimant and Harriet have chosen marriage freely and knowingly, and their witty understanding accommodates a direct and unblinkered knowledge of the dangers facing their love.

There is a final consideration. As long as *The Man of Mode* continues to be virtually ignored in the modern repertory, any argument for its virtues as an important comedy in the dramatic heritage must appear as a piece of special pleading. Plays which fail to hold their place on the stage usually do so for sound theatrical reasons. As long as productions of Restoration comedies were a matter of creating a 'style', based on a vague actorly impression of seventeenth- and eighteenth-century upper-class life, completely unable to distinguish between Congreve and Sheridan, while the producer encouraged hero and heroine to exchange *bons mots* and

[48] Novak, art. cit., places *The Man of Mode* near the conclusion of a debate in the 1670s between Town and Country values. The significance of Harriet's ignorance of Dorimant's relationship with Bellinda was pointed out by Jane Challinor, a postgraduate student at Leeds.

milked the comic figures for laughs, *The Man of Mode*'s episodic plot and dependence on dialogue for action, gave it little chance of success. Now that recent productions have recognized, in William L. Sharp's words, 'that the only possibility of producing [Restoration comedy] successfully is to recognize that we are basically looking at a very realistic picture of the difficulties the sexes have in living with each other . . .',[49] why has *The Man of Mode* received less attention than the work of Wycherley, Congreve, Vanbrugh, and Farquhar?

No doubt part of the explanation is the play's long absence from the stage. Having sustained its popularity during the seventeenth century, it was poorly received in November 1753, and 'much dislik'd and Hiss'd' when it was performed in October 1755.[50] Thereafter it was revived only once in the next twenty years. Effectively, *The Man of Mode* disappeared from the English stage tradition because of the eighteenth-century auditors' moral squeamishness. The number of productions in this century have not been sufficient to regain *The Man of Mode* an audience. Although the comedy requires a large cast of considerable strength, and a set allowing for the Restoration stage's characteristic mixture of intimacy and formality along with quick scene changes and swift exits and entries, a list of recent productions approaches the risible. The Prospect group put the comedy on at the Georgian Theatre, Richmond, in 1965 (calling itself the first production since 1793); it was performed by the English Department at the University of Glasgow in 1966; and by the Royal Shakespeare Company at the Aldwych Theatre in 1971.[51]

Apart from its near-disappearance from the repertory, *The Man of Mode* is at first sight less available to a modern audience. Where Farquhar deals with an emergent but recognizably bourgeois society, and Congreve's comedies give a conventionalized picture of London society (drawing, that is, on earlier comedies so that its realism is tempered by a generalizing tendency), *The Man of Mode* is deeply rooted in the texture of 1676, and its references and word-play might be feared to be too allusive for a modern audience. Nor does Etherege's final play, like *The Country Wife*, offer the possibility of a production approaching a bedroom farce (a view of the play which does Wycherley a severe disservice, but does at least get an audience). So too its Court-based ethos is more distant than that of Vanbrugh's more robust and direct comedy. It would be a pity if the annotation of such matters in this edition, coupled with

[49] 'Restoration Comedy: An Approach to Modern Production', *Drama Survey*, vol. 7 (1968–69), 70–1.
[50] See *The London Stage*, op. cit.
[51] *The Man of Mode*, ed. John Conaghan (Edinburgh, 1973), p. 3.

an insistence upon the way in which the comedy draws strength from its responsiveness to contemporary tensions, should have the effect of making *The Man of Mode* more remote. The strength of Etherege's play is directly related to its close observation of sexual mores at a specific point in time. But because it discerns a coherent patterning within the seeming chaos of contemporary behaviour, those patterns will make themselves apparent in a sensitively performed production of the play.

The modern producer of *The Man of Mode* needs a lack of fearfulness, and a willingness to respond to the rules of the play's world as presented in the text. This needs to be allied to a lack of condescension, and the courage to allow the play to speak for itself. An audience will quickly adjust to the grammar and vocabulary of the game of love presented by the comedy. The problem of how to handle Dorimant also means that a producer has a challenging interpretative freedom to present it as anything between a tolerant romp and a bleakly divisive comedy. In my view it is neither, but until *The Man of Mode*'s challenge is taken up all such arguments will take place in the study. It is difficult to avoid the feeling that contemporary directors and producers have failed the play rather than that the play has failed the modern stage.

NOTE ON THE TEXT

The Man of Mode presents no complicated textual difficulties. It was licensed for publication on 3 June 1676, and entered in the Stationers' Register on 15 June. The first edition, printed by John Macock for Henry Herringman, is a quarto, spaciously and well printed in comparison with many Restoration editions of plays. It collates A–N⁴, and is the only text with any authority. Judging by internal evidence, it derives from Etherege's manuscript rather than a playhouse copy (for example, 'Young' Bellair is not distinguished from 'Old' Bellair until Act II, and in some places stage directions are lacking).

A second quarto of 1684 (Q2) is based on Q1, but introduces minor errors followed by the quarto of 1693 (Q3), which was published two years after Etherege's death. The text given in *The Collected Plays* of 1704 (W) was set up from Q1, again making unimportant changes, mostly for the worse. There are no signs of authorial intervention in any of these later texts, and Q1 must provide the basis for a modern text.

The copy in the Brotherton Collection, University of Leeds, is the copy-text for this edition. Collation with five other copies[1] revealed an uncorrected state in the outer forme of G, not present in any of the twelve copies examined by John Conaghan.[2] As he first discovered, two substantive alterations in the outer forme of I, which occur in a Bodleian copy (Ashmole 1040 (1)) and one of the Worcester College copies (Plays 5.38), are of particular interest. The phrase 'to an English Dancer' is inserted in corrected copies at IV.i, 287 as if it were part of Sir Fopling's speech. Conaghan shrewdly suggests this is in fact meant as a stage direction, and I have adopted this emendation (see Textual Note). This correction, along with the removal of 'had' (l. 290), resembles the kind of change an author might make, but is probably to be accounted for by foul copy or a failure in communication between proof-reader

[1] Bodleian Library (Malone 107 (7), which lacks pp. 95ff., and Ashmole 1401 (1)), Worcester College Library (Plays 5.38 and 7.20), and the Victoria and Albert Museum (Dyce copy).

[2] For a full record and discussion of the other press variants, see *The Man of Mode*, ed. John Conaghan (Edinburgh, 1973), pp. 12–13 and Textual Notes. None of the press variants in the Brotherton copy are significant, but they are worth recording for the sake of completeness—'beliès' for 'bellès' (III.ii, 132; G1), '*Equipage*' for '*Equipage.*' (III.iii, 138 s.d.; G4ᵛ), 'Hey.' for 'Hey,' (III.iii, 138; G4ᵛ).

and compositor. Even if Etherege were involved, the text as a whole indicates that he read proofs with some carelessness.

A peculiarity of Q1 is that it prints Etherege's prose in the form of rough verse. Although his sentences are antithetically patterned, they do not fall into a loose blank verse (as, for instance, Vanbrugh's do in parts of *The Relapse* (1697)). In all probability, Q1 follows the lineation of Etherege's manuscripts, giving each line an initial capital. As Conaghan notes, Thomas Southerne's *The Wives' Excuse* (1692) supplies convincing proof that this layout originated in the printing-shop—half the play is in 'verse', half in prose, and each half was printed at a different shop. This edition therefore treats the play as being written in prose.

The major decision in modernizing the comedy concerns the spelling and accentuation of French words and phrases. In the early editions the spelling of French words is as eccentric as the placing of accents, and might be thought to be an indication of Sir Fopling's ignorance and mispronunciation. There are several arguments against this. No clear pattern emerges, the wits, as well as Sir Fopling, would be guilty of a similar degree of ignorance, and Restoration play-quartos regularly treat French in this way ('deux' for 'doux'). Further, as Carnochan observes, 'If Sir Fopling's French is lame, he becomes a character of farce' instead of a fool whom, Dryden's Epilogue says, the ladies might mistake for a wit.[3] French words have been corrected and modernized throughout, and Sir Fopling presented as foolish and pretentious, but no dunce.

A delicate problem is caused by the large number of words recently imported from the French. Some of these were in the process of being naturalized, and it is not always possible to distinguish between those which would have been accepted as English in 1676, and those felt to be French. The matter is the more complicated since acceptance of such words would have varied among different generations and different classes. Although it is hardly a satisfactory answer, the *OED* has normally been followed in modernizing. On one occasion it seems necessary to distinguish between a newly accepted importation and its French root: see dishabille (II.ii, 76) and *déshabillé* (IV.ii, 105) and notes.

Variant texts of Dryden's Epilogue exist, two in the British Library (MSS. Sloane 203, f. 95, and 1485 f. 23) and one in the Bodleian (MS. Don. b. 8, pp. 558–9). The text of Q1 is independent of these versions, which are collated in *The Works of John Dryden*, ed. E. N. Hooker and H. T. Swedenberg (Berkeley and Los Angeles, 1956–), vol. 1, 397–8. One reading ('it' for 'they', l.

[3] *The Man of Mode*, ed. W. B. Carnochan (Lincoln, Nebraska, 1966, London, 1967), p. ix n.

6) has been adopted, but the others, including an additional couplet, ignored (for details, see Textual Note).

All substantive departures from the copy-text are given in the Textual Notes, along with some of the more interesting variants from Q1-3 and W. The decisions of four important modern editors, Verity, Brett-Smith, Carnochan, and Conaghan, are also recorded where significant (when a variant is given, all later editions follow Q1 unless otherwise noted). The handling of punctuation is indebted to Carnochan's, though his changes, generally tactful, are not followed where Q1, Verity, or some alternative arrangement seems preferable. In modernizing some silent alterations have been made. Names and abbreviations of names have been normalized, expanded, and capitalized in speech prefixes and stage directions; some stage directions have been shifted slightly in the interests of clarity; typographical slips have been corrected; spellings have been modernized according to the *OED*; some words have been modernized (e.g., 'ungrateful' for 'ingrateful'); and contractions in the dialogue ('H'as', 'th' next','wo'not', etc.) have been either expanded ('He has') if the cadence or emphasis demands it, or given in modernized form ('He's', 'won't'). Etherege regularly gives Hyde Park and the Mall as 'High Park' and the 'Mail', but these forms have been modernized throughout: no modern production would employ either on the stage, even though it reflects Etherege's intentions (see notes to III.iii, 34 and II.ii, 158). All editorial insertions are marked by square brackets.

Sir Car Scroope's song ('As Amoret with Phillis sat') in Act V, Scene ii, has sometimes been attributed to Etherege or Sedley in error. Two other songs, 'Caelia with mournful pleasure hears' and 'That you alone my Heart possess', are falsely identified as songs from *The Man of Mode* (*The Poems of Sir George Etherege*, ed. James Thorpe (Princeton, 1963), pp. 144–5).

FURTHER READING

Editions

The Dramatic Works of Sir George Etherege, ed. H. F. B. Brett-Smith, 2 vols. (Oxford, 1927).

The Letterbook of Sir George Etherege, ed. Sybil Rosenfeld (Oxford, 1928).

Letters of Sir George Etherege, ed. Frederick Bracher (Berkeley, Los Angeles, London, 1974).

The Poems of Sir George Etherege, ed. James Thorpe (Princeton, N.J., 1963).

Critical Works

Berman, Ronald. 'The Comic Passions of *The Man of Mode*', Studies in English Literature, 1500–*1900*, vol. 10 (1970), 459–68.

Davies, Paul C. 'The State of Nature and the State of War: A Reconsideration of *The Man of Mode*', *University of Toronto Quarterly*, vol. 39 (1969), 53–62.

Dennis, John. *A Defense of Sir Fopling Flutter* (1722), in *The Critical Works of John Dennis*, ed. E. N. Hooker, 2 vols. (Baltimore, 1939–43).

Fujimura, Thomas H. *The Restoration Comedy of Wit* (Princeton, 1952).

Hawkins, Harriet. Chapter on *The Man of Mode* in *Likenesses of Truth in Elizabethan and Restoration Comedy* (Oxford, 1972).

Hayman, John G. 'Dorimant and the Comedy of A Man of Mode', *Modern Language Quarterly*, vol. 30 (1969), 183–97.

Holland, Norman N. *The First Modern Comedies: The Significance of Etherege, Wycherley and Congreve* (Cambridge, Mass., 1959).

Hume, Robert D. *The Development of English Drama in the late Seventeenth Century* (Oxford, 1976).

——'The Myth of the Rake in "Restoration" Comedy', *Studies in the Literary Imagination*, vol. 10 (1977), 25–55.

Knights, L. C. 'Restoration Comedy: The Reality and the Myth', *Explorations* (London, 1946).

Krause, David. 'The Defaced Angel: A Concept of Satanic Grace in Etherege's *The Man of Mode*', *Drama Survey*, vol. 7 (1969), 87–103.

Leech, Clifford. 'Restoration Comedy: The Earlier Phase', *Essays in Criticism*, vol. 1 (1951), 165–84.

Lynch, Kathleen. *The Social Mode of Restoration Comedy,* University of Michigan Publications, *Language and Literature*, vol. 3 (New York and London, 1926).

Novak, Maximillian. 'Margery Pinchwife's "London Disease": Restoration Comedy and the Libertine Offensive of the 1670's', *Studies in the Literary Imagination*, vol. 10 (1977), 1–25.

Powell, Jocelyn. 'George Etherege and the Form of a Comedy', *Stratford-upon-Avon Studies 6, Restoration Theatre* (London, 1965).

Scouten, Arthur H. 'Plays and Playwrights' in *The Revels History of Drama in English*, vol. 5 *1660–1750*, ed. T. W. Craik (1976).

Steele, Sir Richard. *The Spectator*, No. 65 (15 May 1711).

Underwood, Dale. *Etherege and the Seventeenth-Century Comedy of Manners* (New Haven, Conn., 1957).

Walpole, Horace. 'Thoughts on Comedy; written in 1775 and 1776', in *The Works* (1798), vol. 2, 315–22.

ABBREVIATIONS

B   *The Dramatic Works of Sir George Etherege*, ed. H. F. B. Brett-Smith (Oxford, 1927).

CA   *The Man of Mode*, ed. W. B. Carnochan, Regents Restoration Drama Series (Lincoln, Neb., London, 1966, 1967).

CO   *The Man of Mode*, ed. John Conaghan, Fountainwell Drama Series (Edinburgh, 1973).

Q1   *The Man of Mode* (1676). Quarto.

Q2   *The Man of Mode* (1684). Quarto.

Q3   *The Man of Mode* (1693). Quarto.

Thorpe   *The Poems of Sir George Etherege*, ed. James Thorpe (Princeton, N.J., 1963).

V   *The Works of Sir George Etherege*, ed. A. W. Verity (1888).

W   *The Works of Sir George Etherege* (1704). Octavo.

M.E.   Middle English

N & Q *Notes and Queries*

OED   *Oxford English Dictionary*

obs.   obsolescent usage

s.d.   stage direction

var.   variant

THE
Man of Mode,
OR,
Sᴿ Fopling Flutter.
A
COMEDY.

Acted at the *Duke's Theatre.*

By *George Etherege* Esq;.

LICENSED,

June 3.
1676.

Roger L'Estrange.

LONDON,

Printed by *J. Macock*, for *Henry Herringman*, at the Sign of
the *Blew Anchor* in the Lower Walk of the
New Exchange, 1 6 7 6.

TO HER ROYAL HIGHNESS
THE DUCHESS

MADAM,

Poets, however they may be modest otherwise, have always too good an opinion of what they write. The world, when it sees this play dedicated to your Royal Highness, will conclude I have more than my share of that vanity. But I hope the honour I have of 5 belonging to you will excuse my presumption. 'Tis the first thing I have produced in your service, and my duty obliges me to what my choice durst not else have aspired.

I am very sensible, Madam, how much it is beholding to your indulgence for the success it had in the acting, and your protection 10 will be no less fortunate to it in the printing; for all are so ambitious of making their court to you, that none can be severe to what you are pleased to favour.

This universal submission and respect is due to the greatness of your rank and birth; but you have other illustrious qualities which 15 are much more engaging. Those would but dazzle, did not these really charm the eyes and understandings of all who have the happiness to approach you.

Authors on these occasions are never wanting to publish a particular of their patron's virtues and perfections; but your Royal 20 Highness's are so eminently known that, did I follow their examples, I should but paint those wonders here of which everyone already has the idea in his mind. Besides, I do not think it proper to aim at that in prose which is so glorious a subject for verse, in which

---

9 *sensible* aware
9 *beholding* Q1 (beholden W)

Her ... Duchess Mary Beatrice of Modena (1658–1718), became Duchess of York in 1673. On her husband's accession as James II she became Queen.
7 *service ... duty* this is the only evidence that Etherege served the Duchess in some capacity at this date. Gildon reported that she held the dramatist 'in particular esteem'. In 1682 her husband gave Etherege a pension of £100 and, as King, appointed him envoy to the Diet at Ratisbon in 1685. That appointment was due to the good offices of Lord Sunderland rather than the Queen as Gildon claimed (*The Letterbook of Sir George Etherege*, ed. Sybil Rosenfeld (1928), pp. 15–16). What form the Duchess's 'indulgence' (l.10) took in helping the comedy's success on the stage is not known.

hereafter if I show more zeal than skill, it will not grieve me much,   25
since I less passionately desire to be esteemed a poet than to be
thought,

       Madam,
          Your Royal Highness's
             most humble, most obedient,   30
             and most faithful servant,

                             GEORGE ETHEREGE

PROLOGUE

By Sir Car Scroope, Baronet

Like dancers on the ropes poor poets fare:
Most perish young, the rest in danger are.
This, one would think, should make our authors wary,
But, gamester-like, the giddy fools miscarry;
A lucky hand or two so tempts 'em on,   5
They cannot leave off play till they're undone.
With modest fears a Muse does first begin,
Like a young wench newly enticed to sin;
But tickled once with praise, by her good will,
The wanton fool would never more lie still.   10
'Tis an old mistress you'll meet here tonight,
Whose charms you once looked on with delight.
But now, of late, such dirty drabs have known ye,
A Muse o'the better sort's ashamed to own ye.
Nature well-drawn and wit must now give place   15
To gaudy nonsense and to dull grimace;
Nor is it strange that you should like so much
That kind of wit, for most of yours is such.
But I'm afraid that while to France we go,
To bring you home fine dresses, dance, and show,   20
The stage, like you, will but more foppish grow.
Of foreign wares why should we fetch the scum,
When we can be so richly served at home?
For, heav'n be thanked, 'tis not so wise an age
But your own follies may supply the stage.   25
Though often ploughed, there's no great fear the soil
Should barren grow by the too-frequent toil,
While at your doors are to be daily found
Such loads of dunghill to manure the ground.
'Tis by your follies that we players thrive,   30
As the physicians by diseases live;
And as each year some new distemper reigns,

9 *will* puns on the name, Will
13 *drab* slatternly woman or prostitute
14 *ye* Q2–3, V, CA (you Q1)

Sir Car Scroope wit, courtier, and poet (1649–80). He wrote Dorimant's song in V.ii.

5

Whose friendly poison helps t'increase their gains,
So, among you, there starts up every day
Some new, unheard-of fool for us to play.   35
Then, for your own sakes, be not too severe,
Nor what you all admire at home, damn here.
Since each is fond of his own ugly face,
Why should you, when we hold it, break the glass?

33 *t' increase* Q2–3, W, V, CA (to increase Q1)

DRAMATIS PERSONAE

MR DORIMANT
MR MEDLEY [*his friend*]
OLD BELLAIR   *Gentlemen*
YOUNG BELLAIR [*his son, in love with Emilia*]
SIR FOPLING FLUTTER   5
LADY TOWNLEY [*sister of Old Bellair*]
EMILIA
MRS LOVEIT [*in love with Dorimant*]
BELLINDA [*in love with Dorimant*]   *Gentlewomen*
LADY WOODVILL, *and*
HARRIET, *her daughter*   10
PERT
and   *Waiting women*
BUSY
A SHOEMAKER   15
AN ORANGE-WOMAN
FOUR SLOVENLY BULLIES
TWO CHAIRMEN
MR SMIRK, *a parson*
HANDY, *a valet de chambre*   20
PAGES, FOOTMEN, *etc.*

---

17 FOUR ed. (*Three* Q1)

---

17 FOUR ... BULLIES see notes to III.iii, 201 s.d.
20 *valet de chambre* see note to IV.ii, 98

THE MAN OF MODE,
or,
Sir Fopling Flutter
a Comedy

Act I

A dressing room. A table covered with a toilet; clothes laid ready.

Enter DORIMANT *in his gown and slippers, with a note in his hand made up, repeating verses*

DORIMANT

'Now, for some ages, had the pride of Spain
Made the sun shine on half the world in vain'.

Then looking on the note

'For Mrs Loveit'. What a dull, insipid thing is a billet doux written in cold blood after the heat of the business is over! It is a tax upon good nature which I have here been labouring to pay, and have   5
done it, but with as much regret as ever fanatic paid the Royal Aid or church duties. 'Twill have the same fate, I know, that all my notes to her have had of late—'twill not be thought kind enough. Faith, women are i' the right when they jealously examine our

---

1 s.d. *made up* normally means sealed up, but see I, 173 ff.
3 *'For Mrs Loveit'* CA (Q1, etc., centre above Dorimant's speech without quotation marks)

---

1 s.d. *toilet* cloth cover for a dressing-table, of rich material and workmanship. *OED* cites *London Gazette* (1683), No. 1811/4: 'Stolen the 20th Instant, a Toilet of blew Velvet, with a Gold and Silver Fringe'.
1–2 *Now ... vain* opening couplet of Waller's 'Of a War with Spain, and a Fight at Sea' (*Poems*, ed. G. Thorn Drury (1901), vol. 2, 23). John Dennis reported that contemporaries, in identifying Rochester with Dorimant, instanced his 'repeating, on every Occasion, the Verses of *Waller*, for whom that noble Lord had a very particular Esteem' (*Defence of Sir Fopling Flutter* (1722) in *Critical Works*, ed. E. N. Hooker (Baltimore, Md., 1939–42), vol. 2, 248).
6 *fanatic* in the latter part of the seventeenth century a hostile epithet applied to Nonconformists. *OED* cites John Gaule (1657), 'Enthusiasts, Anabaptists, Fanaticks, and Familists'. Nonconformists opposed both the Crown and the established Church.
6–7 *Royal Aid ... church duties* 'Royal Aid' was an extraordinary subsidy or tax made by Parliament for the King. Church duties were levied locally for the services of the parish church.

9

letters, for in them we always first discover our decay of 10
passion.—Hey! Who waits?

Enter HANDY

HANDY
Sir—
DORIMANT
Call a footman.
HANDY
None of 'em are come yet.
DORIMANT
Dogs! Will they ever lie snoring abed till noon?   15
HANDY
'Tis all one, sir: if they're up, you indulge 'em so, they're ever
poaching after whores all the morning.
DORIMANT
Take notice henceforward who's wanting in his duty—the next
clap he gets, he shall rot for an example. What vermin are those
chattering without?   20
HANDY
Foggy Nan, the orange-woman, and swearing Tom, the
shoemaker.
DORIMANT
Go, call in that overgrown jade with the flasket of guts before
her. Fruit is refreshing in a morning.

Exit HANDY

'It is not that I love you less,   25
   Than when before your feet I lay—'

Enter ORANGE-WOMAN [*and* HANDY]

How now, double-tripe, what news do you bring?
ORANGE-WOMAN
News! Here's the best fruit has come to town t' year. Gad, I was
up before four o'clock this morning and bought all the choice i'
the market.   30

---

21 *Foggy* unwholesomely bloated, puffy
23 *flasket* 'a long shallow basket' (Johnson), or, possibly, a small flask

---

17 *poaching after* taking game illegally (which carries on the hunting imagery), but
    possibly containing a sexual pun on the meaning 'poke' (from OF *pocher*, to
    thrust or dig out with the fingers).
25–6 *It . . . lay* Waller, 'The Self-Banished', ll. 1–2 (*Poems*, ed. G. Thorn Drury
    (1901), vol. 1, 101).

DORIMANT

The nasty refuse of your shop.

ORANGE-WOMAN

You need not make mouths at it. I assure you, 'tis all culled ware.

DORIMANT

The citizens buy better on a holiday in their walk to Tot'nam.

ORANGE-WOMAN

Good or bad, 'tis all one; I never knew you commend anything.
Lord, would the ladies had heard you talk of 'em as I have done.   35
Here—

Sets down the fruit

Bid your man give me an angel.

DORIMANT [*to* HANDY]

Give the bawd her fruit again.

ORANGE-WOMAN

Well, on my conscience, there never was the like of you—God's
my life, I had almost forgot to tell you, there is a young gentle-   40
woman, lately come to town with her mother, that is so taken
with you.

DORIMANT

Is she handsome?

ORANGE-WOMAN

Nay, gad, there are few finer women, I tell you but so, and a
hugeous fortune, they say. Here, eat this peach, it comes from   45
the stone. 'Tis better than any Newington you've tasted.

DORIMANT

This fine woman, I'll lay my life (*taking the peach*), is some
awkward, ill-fashioned country toad, who, not having above
four dozen of black hairs on her head, has adorned her baldness

33 *citizens ... Tot'nam* Tottenham then lay some 4 miles north of the suburbs
beginning to grow outside the City, and so was convenient for tradespeople's
outings. Shadwell distinguishes the different classes of Londoner in *The Vir-
tuoso* (1676)—'your Glass-Coach will to *Hide-Park* for Air. The Suburb-fools
trudge to *Lamb's-Conduit* or *Totnam*; your sprucer sort of Citizens gallop to
Epsom; your Mechanick gross Fellows, shewing much conjugal affection, strut
before their Wives, each with a Child in his Arms, to *Islington*, or *Hogsdon*'
(*Complete Works*, ed. M. Summers (1927), vol. 3, 164).

37 *angel* gold coin, originally called angel-noble, with the archangel Michael and
the dragon as its device. Its value varied from 6*s*. 8*d*. to 10*s*.

38 *bawd* fruit-women were well-known go-betweens. Conaghan cites Dryden's
The Assignation (1673), 'Why, if you will have it, you are little better than a
procuress: you carry messages betwixt party and party, and, in one word Sir,
she's as arrant a Fruit-woman as any is about *Rome*' (*Dramatic Works*, ed. M.
Summers (1931–32), vol. 3, 303).

45–6 *peach ... Newington* presumably a variety of peach from Newington, Kent.
The flesh of a freestone (as opposed to clingstone) separates from the stone.

with a large white fruz, that she may look sparkishly in the   50
forefront of the King's box at an old play.

ORANGE-WOMAN

Gad, you'd change your note quickly if you did but see her!

DORIMANT

How came she to know me?

ORANGE-WOMAN

She saw you yesterday at the Change. She told me you came and
fooled with the woman at the next shop.   55

DORIMANT

I remember, there was a mask observed me, indeed. Fooled, did
she say?

ORANGE-WOMAN

Ay; I vow she told me twenty things you said too, and acted with
her head and with her body so like you—

Enter MEDLEY

MEDLEY

Dorimant, my life, my joy, my darling sin! How dost thou?   60
[*Embraces him*]

ORANGE-WOMAN

Lord, what a filthy trick these men have got of kissing one
another!   *She spits*

58–9 *with her head* W, V, B, CA (with head Q1)
59 *like* Q1 (W, V omit)

---

50 *fruz* clearly means a wig with short curled hair. Not recorded in *OED* which
   gives 'fruz' as meaning 'A collection of short and small branches, producing a
   frizzy appearance'. However, there are several contemporary examples of the
   word as a verb meaning 'to frizz out the hair'. Thackeray uses 'fuzz-wig' (1848).

50 *sparkishly* a rare adverb: *OED* cites four examples, of which this is the earliest.
   When used of a woman, 'spark' meant one of great beauty, elegance, or wit.
   Applied to a man it is usually depreciative, and meant a young man of elegant or
   foppish character.

54 *Change* the New Exchange, an arcade on the south side of the Strand, with two
   long double galleries of shops, one above the other. Etherege had used it as a
   setting in *She Wou'd if She Cou'd*, III.i. Fashionable London bought ribbons,
   knots, and essences there; consequently lodgings in the Strand over against the
   Exchange were popular with country visitors (see Bellinda's remarks at V.i,
   48–51). Brett-Smith points out that Herringman, Etherege's publisher, had
   his shop there.

61–2 *a filthy trick . . . another* (compare with IV.i, 184). Shadwell's *Sullen Lovers*
   (1668) gives a further example of this exaggerated custom when Woodcock is
   described as 'A Familiar loving Coxcombe, that embraces and kisses all men
   . . .'

MEDLEY

Why do you suffer this cartload of scandal to come near you and make your neighbours think you so improvident to need a bawd?

ORANGE-WOMAN [*to* DORIMANT]

Good, now we shall have it! You did but want him to help you.   65
Come, pay me for my fruit.

MEDLEY

Make us thankful for it, huswife. Bawds are as much out of fashion as gentlemen-ushers: none but old formal ladies use the one, and none but foppish old stagers employ the other. Go, you are an insignificant brandy bottle.   70

DORIMANT

Nay, there you wrong her. Three quarts of canary is her business.

ORANGE-WOMAN

What you please, gentlemen.

DORIMANT

To him! Give him as good as he brings.

ORANGE-WOMAN

Hang him, there is not such another heathen in the town again,   75
except it be the shoemaker without.

MEDLEY

I shall see you hold up your hand at the bar next sessions for murder, huswife. That shoemaker can take his oath you are in fee with the doctors to sell green fruit to the gentry, that the crudities may breed diseases.   80

ORANGE-WOMAN

Pray give me my money.

DORIMANT

Not a penny! When you bring the gentlewoman hither you spoke of, you shall be paid.

ORANGE-WOMAN

The gentlewoman! The gentlewoman may be as honest as your

---

65 *Good ... You* V, CA (Good now, we shall have it, you Q1; Good now, we shall have it; you Q3; Good, now we shall have it, you W)
65 *want* need
69 *stagers* Q1 (strangers W, V) veterans, old hands
80 *crudities* undigested (or indigestible) matter in the stomach
84 *honest* honourable, chaste

---

71 *canary* a light sweet wine from the Canary Islands. Visitors to the bawdy houses of the day were usually put to the expense of a few bottles of wine. Possibly there is also a pun on the abbreviation of thieves' slang, 'canary-bird'—'a Rogue or Whore taken, and clapp'd into the Cage or Round-house' (*A New Canting Dictionary* (1725)).

sisters, for aught as I know. Pray pay me, Mr Dorimant, and do   85
not abuse me so. I have an honester way of living—you know it.

MEDLEY
Was there ever such a resty bawd?

DORIMANT
Some jade's tricks she has, but she makes amends when she's in
good humour. Come, tell me the lady's name, and Handy shall
pay you.   90

ORANGE-WOMAN
I must not, she forbid me.

DORIMANT
That's a sure sign she would have you.

MEDLEY
Where does she live?

ORANGE-WOMAN
They lodge at my house.

MEDLEY
Nay, then she's in a hopeful way.   95

ORANGE-WOMAN
Good Mr Medley, say your pleasure of me, but take heed how
you affront my house. God's my life, in a hopeful way!

DORIMANT
Prithee, peace. What kind of woman's the mother?

ORANGE-WOMAN
A goodly, grave gentlewoman. Lord, how she talks against the
wild young men o' the town! As for your part, she thinks you an   100
arrant devil: should she see you, on my conscience she would
look if you had not a cloven foot.

DORIMANT
Does she know me?

ORANGE-WOMAN
Only by hearsay. A thousand horrid stories have been told her of
you, and she believes 'em all.   105

MEDLEY
By the character, this should be the famous Lady Woodvill and
her daughter Harriet.

ORANGE-WOMAN [aside]
The devil's in him for guessing, I think.

85 *sisters* Q1 (sister W, V)   87 *resty* restive or indolent, sluggish
88 *jade* contemptuous name for an inferior horse, applied pejoratively to women
98 *Prithee* I pray thee

---

100 *wild* see Introduction, pp. xxix–xxxi.
101 *arrant* (a) wandering, as in 'knight errant', hence with the sense of genuine, (b)
    downright or manifest, and hence, unmitigated.

DORIMANT

Do you know 'em?

MEDLEY

Both very well. The mother's a great admirer of the forms and   110
civility of the last age.

DORIMANT

An antiquated beauty may be allowed to be out of humour at the
freedoms of the present. This is a good account of the mother.
Pray, what is the daughter?

MEDLEY

Why, first, she's an heiress, vastly rich.   115

DORIMANT

And handsome?

MEDLEY

What alteration a twelvemonth may have bred in her, I know
not, but a year ago she was the beautifullest creature I ever
saw—a fine, easy, clean shape, light brown hair in abundance,
her features regular, her complexion clear, and lively, large,   120
wanton eyes; but, above all, a mouth that has made me kiss it
a thousand times in imagination—teeth white and even, and
pretty, pouting lips, with a little moisture ever hanging on them,
that look like the Provence rose fresh on the bush, ere the
morning sun has quite drawn up the dew.   125

---

111 *civility* Q1 (civilities Q2–3)
124 *Provence* V (Province Q1; Provins CA)

110–11 *forms and civility of the last age* i.e., the manners and social decorum of the
previous generation (those of Charles I's Court). 'Forms' carries the sense of a
set method of outward behaviour according with etiquette. *OED* gives its last
example of 'forms' meaning 'manners' from 1639, but it is common in Restoration comedy, usually in a pejorative sense and with an old-fashioned flavour.
See Lady Wishfort, *The Way of the World* (1700), III.i., 'I shall never break
Decorums . . . I hope Sir *Rowland* is better bred, than to put a Lady to the
necessity of breaking her Forms'.

119 *easy* a word carrying several meanings in the play. See Introduction, p. xxxiii.
Here (as at III.iii, 28) the sense is graceful, attractive (a meaning not recorded
in *OED*).

121 *wanton* the meaning goes beyond Carnochan's 'lively, roguish'. Medley's libertine values set the wide range of the word's senses in tension. At the primary
level, Harriet's eyes are sexually alive and playful. The context inverts the
morally condemnatory sense of lascivious, unchaste, and remembers other
meanings—free, unrestrained (poet.); capricious, giddy; reckless of decorum.

124 *Provence rose* the cabbage rose (*rosa centifolia*). 'The misnamed Provence rose
was first introduced into France by the Crusaders at Provins (Seine and
Marne)' (*Westminster Gazette*, 31 July 1905). Carnochan emends to 'Provins
rose', now used to describe *rosa gallica*.

DORIMANT
  Rapture, mere rapture!
ORANGE-WOMAN
  Nay, gad, he tells you true. She's a delicate creature.
DORIMANT
  Has she wit?
MEDLEY
  More than is usual in her sex, and as much malice. Then, she's as
  wild as you would wish her, and has a demureness in her looks   130
  that makes it so surprising.
DORIMANT
  Flesh and blood cannot hear this and not long to know her.
MEDLEY
  I wonder what makes her mother bring her up to town? An old,
  doting keeper cannot be more jealous of his mistress.
ORANGE-WOMAN
  She made me laugh yesterday. There was a judge came to visit   135
  'em, and the old man (she told me) did so stare upon her and,
  when he saluted her, smacked so heartily—who would think it of
  'em?
MEDLEY
  God-a-mercy, Judge!
DORIMANT
  Do 'em right, the gentlemen of the long robe have not been   140
  wanting by their good examples to countenance the crying sin o'
  the nation.
MEDLEY
  Come, on with your trappings; 'tis later than you imagine.
DORIMANT
  Call in the shoemaker, Handy!
ORANGE-WOMAN
  Good Mr Dorimant, pay me. Gad, I had rather give you my fruit   145
  than stay to be abused by that foul-mouthed rogue. What you
  gentlemen say, it matters not much, but such a dirty fellow does
  one more disgrace.
DORIMANT [to HANDY]
  Give her ten shillings. [To ORANGE-WOMAN] And be sure you tell
  the young gentlewoman I must be acquainted with her.   150

126 *mere* pure, sheer
139 *Judge* Q1 (a judge V)
140 *gentlemen ... robe* members of the legal profession

---

130 *wild* see Introduction, pp. xxix–xxxi.
139 *God-a-mercy* 'God reward you', hence used as an exclamation of thanks (here
  ironically).

ORANGE-WOMAN

Now do you long to be tempting this pretty creature. Well,
heavens mend you!

MEDLEY

Farewell, bog!   *Exeunt* ORANGE-WOMAN *and* HANDY
Dorimant, when did you see your *pis aller*, as you call her, Mrs
Loveit?   155

DORIMANT

Not these two days.

MEDLEY

And how stand affairs between you?

DORIMANT

There has been great patching of late, much ado—we make a
shift to hang together.

MEDLEY

I wonder how her mighty spirit bears it?   160

DORIMANT

Ill enough, on all conscience. I never knew so violent a creature.

MEDLEY

She's the most passionate in her love and the most extravagant in
her jealousy of any woman I ever heard of. What note is that?

DORIMANT

An excuse I am going to send her for the neglect I am guilty of.

MEDLEY

Prithee, read it.   165

DORIMANT

No, but if you will take the pains, you may.

MEDLEY (*reads*)

'I never was a lover of business, but now I have a just reason to
hate it, since it has kept me these two days from seeing you. I
intend to wait upon you in the afternoon, and in the pleasure of
your conversation forget all I have suffered during this tedious   170
absence'.—This business of yours, Dorimant, has been with a

---

153 *bog* bugbear (*OED*, sb. 2, cites this example)
154 *pis aller* last resource, makeshift
158 *late ... we* V, B, CA, CO (late, much Ado we Q1; late; with much ado we Q3)

---

162 *extravagant* see Introduction, pp. xxxi–iii.
170 *conversation* although the word carries the more limited modern meaning, it
     includes the idea of social intimacy. Medley may be playing on a further
     meaning, sexual intercourse.

vizard at the playhouse; I have had an eye on you. If some
malicious body should betray you, this kind note would hardly
make your peace with her.

DORIMANT

I desire no better.   175

MEDLEY

Why, would her knowledge of it oblige you?

DORIMANT

Most infinitely; next to the coming to a good understanding with
a new mistress, I love a quarrel with an old one. But the devil's
in't, there has been such a calm in my affairs of late, I have not
had the pleasure of making a woman so much as break her fan, to   180
be sullen, or forswear herself, these three days.

MEDLEY

A very great misfortune! Let me see, I love mischief well enough
to forward this business myself. I'll about it presently, and
though I know the truth of what you've done, will set her
a-raving. I'll heighten it a little with invention, leave her in a fit o'   185
the mother, and be here again before you're ready.

DORIMANT

Pray, stay; you may spare yourself the labour. The business is
undertaken already by one who will manage it with as much
address and, I think, with a little more malice than you can.

MEDLEY

Who i' the devil's name can this be?   190

DORIMANT

Why, the vizard, that very vizard you saw me with.

MEDLEY

Does she love mischief so well as to betray herself to spite
another?

DORIMANT

Not so neither, Medley; I will make you comprehend the
mystery. This mask, for a farther confirmation of what I have   195
been these two days swearing to her, made me yesterday at the
playhouse make her a promise, before her face, utterly to break

172 *vizard* mask, hence a woman wearing a mask; often used of a masked prostitute.
Masks were fashionable in the early Restoration period, but fell into disfavour
because of their use by courtezans. In *She Wou'd if She Cou'd* (1668), III.iii, Mr
Rakehell, 'a Knight of the Industry', is expected with a 'Coach full or two of
Vizard-masks and silk Petticoates'.

186 *mother* hysteria. Compare *King Lear*, II.iv, 56–7, 'O! how this mother swells
up toward my heart, /*Hysterica passio!* down . . .' Kenneth Muir cites Edward
Jordan (1605): '. . . the Mother of the Suffocation of the Mother, because, most
commonly, it takes them with choking in the throat; and it is an affect of the
mother or wombe . . .' (New Arden).

off with Loveit; and because she tenders my reputation and
would not have me do a barbarous thing, has contrived a way to
give me a handsome occasion.　　　　　　　　　　　　　　200

MEDLEY

Very good.

DORIMANT

She intends, about an hour before me this afternoon, to make
Loveit a visit; and having the privilege, by reason of a professed
friendship between 'em, to talk of her concerns—

MEDLEY

Is she a friend?　　　　　　　　　　　　　　　　　　205

DORIMANT

Oh, an intimate friend!

MEDLEY

Better and better! Pray proceed.

DORIMANT

She means insensibly to insinuate a discourse of me, and artificially raise her jealousy to such a height that, transported with
the first motions of her passion, she shall fly upon me with all the　210
fury imaginable as soon as ever I enter. The quarrel being thus
happily begun, I am to play my part: confess and justify all my
roguery, swear her impertinence and ill humour makes her
intolerable, tax her with the next fop that comes into my head,
and in a huff march away, slight her, and leave her to be taken by　215
whosoever thinks it worth his time to lie down before her.

MEDLEY

This vizard is a spark, and has a genius that makes her worthy of
yourself, Dorimant.

Enter HANDY, SHOEMAKER, *and* FOOTMAN

DORIMANT [*to* FOOTMAN]

You rogue there, who sneak like a dog that has flung down a dish,
if you do not mend your waiting, I'll uncase you and turn you　220
loose to the wheel of fortune.—Handy, seal this and let him run
with it presently.

Exeunt HANDY *and* FOOTMAN [: HANDY *re-enters after a few*
　　　　　　　　　　　　　　　　　　　　moments]

198 *tenders* regards, treats with tenderness
204 *'em, to . . . concerns*—Q1 ('em) to . . . concerns. W, V)
208–9 *artificially* artfully　　　　　　　　217 *genius* prevailing character or spirit
220 *uncase you* strip you (of your livery)　　222 *presently* immediately
222 s.d. *Exeunt . . . moments*] ed. (*Exeunt . . .* FOOTMAN Q1; *Exit Footman* CA)

---

222 s.d. *Exeunt . . .* FOOTMAN Handy leaves with the footman to seal the note, but
　　returns before l. 272. His entry is unmarked, but there is no need to emend with
　　Carnochan (see above).

MEDLEY

Since you're resolved on a quarrel, why do you send her this kind note?

DORIMANT

To keep her at home in order to the business. (*To the* 225 SHOEMAKER) How now, you drunken sot?

SHOEMAKER

'Zbud, you have no reason to talk. I have not had a bottle of sack of yours in my belly this fortnight.

MEDLEY

The orange-woman says your neighbours take notice what a heathen you are, and design to inform the bishop and have you 230 burned for an atheist.

SHOEMAKER

Damn her, dunghill! If her husband does not remove her, she stinks so, the parish intend to indict him for a nuisance.

MEDLEY

I advise you like a friend, reform your life. You have brought the envy of the world upon you by living above yourself. Whoring 235 and swearing are vices too genteel for a shoemaker.

SHOEMAKER

'Zbud, I think you men of quality will grow as unreasonable as the women: you would engross the sins o' the nation. Poor folks can no sooner be wicked but they're railed at by their betters.

DORIMANT

Sirrah, I'll have you stand i' the pillory for this libel.   240

SHOEMAKER

Some of you deserve it, I'm sure. There are so many of 'em that our journeymen nowadays, instead of harmless ballads, sing nothing but your damned lampoons.

DORIMANT

Our lampoons, you rogue?

---

225 *in order to* for the sake of (obs.)   227 *'Zbud* 'Sblood, i.e. 'God's blood'
227 *sack* a class of white wines formerly imported from the Canaries and Spain
238 *engross* monopolize, wholly absorb   242 *harmless* inoffensive

---

242–3 *harmless ballads … your damned lampoons* the city journeymen's traditional taste for popular ballads has been corrupted by the flood of scurrilous satires and lampoons which the Shoemaker identifies with the wits. According to the *OED* 'lampoon' first occurs in 1649. Lampoons and libels circulated widely through manuscript copies in Restoration London, but also found their way into print as well as being sometimes nailed to the victim's door. Etherege himself was regarded as the writer of 'airy songs and soft lampoons' (Thorpe, p. vi).

SHOEMAKER

Nay, good master, why should not you write your own commen- 245
taries as well as Caesar?

MEDLEY

The rascal's read, I perceive.

SHOEMAKER

You know the old proverb—ale and history.

DORIMANT

Draw on my shoes, sirrah.

SHOEMAKER

Here's a shoe—   250

DORIMANT

Sits with more wrinkles than there are in an angry bully's fore-
head.

SHOEMAKER

'Zbud, as smooth as your mistress's skin does upon her. So,
strike your foot in home. 'Zbud, if e'er a monsieur of 'em all make
more fashionable ware, I'll be content to have my ears whipped 255
off with my own paring knife.

MEDLEY

And served up in a ragout, instead of cockcombs, to a company
of French shoemakers for a collation.

SHOEMAKER

Hold, hold! Damn 'em caterpillars! Let 'em feed upon cab-

---

251 *bully* blustering gallant, swashbuckler
257 *ragout* highly flavoured stew
258 *collation* light repast

---

248 *ale and history* 'Truth is in ale as in history' (M. P. Tilley, *A Dictionary of
    Proverbs in England in the Sixteenth and Seventeenth Centuries* (1950), T578).
    But G. L. Apperson, *English Proverbs and Proverbial Phrases* (1929), p. 4,
    regards the evidence as too slight for the sentence to be regarded as a proverb.
    However, the phrase was current in the seventeenth century, occurring in
    Bishop Corbett's *Iter Boreale* (*Poems of Richard Corbett*, ed. J. A. W. Bennett
    and H. R. Trevor-Roper (1955), p. 43), while Fielding quotes an unidentified
    couplet in *Tom Jones*, IV.i.—'While history with her comrade ale, /Soothes the
    sad series of her serious tale'—and also refers to Butler's couplet, 'Thou that
    with Ale, or viler Liquors, /Didst inspire *Withers*, *Pryn* and *Vickars*' (*Hudibras*
    (1663–78), Part I, Canto i, 645–6).
257–8 *ragout . . . collation* cockscombs can be used in French cooking as a garnish or
    in a sauce. The joke was still current in 1733: James Bramston satirizes a
    Frenchified taste for '. . . frogs fricasseed, and coxcomb pies' (*The Man of Taste*,
    p. 14).

bage!—Come master, your health this morning!—next my   260
heart now!

DORIMANT

Go, get you home, and govern your family better! Do not let
your wife follow you to the alehouse, beat your whore, and lead
you home in triumph.

SHOEMAKER

'Zbud, there's never a man i' the town lives more like a gentleman   265
with his wife than I do. I never mind her motions; she never
inquires into mine. We speak to one another civilly, hate one
another heartily, and because 'tis vulgar to lie and soak together,
we have each of us our several settle-bed.

DORIMANT [to HANDY]

Give him half a crown.   270

MEDLEY

Not without he will promise to be bloody drunk.

---

260 *morning!—next* ed. (Morning next Q1, CA; morning! next B)
266 *motions* either, movements, or emotions, inner promptings (obs.)
269 *several* separate
269 *settle-bed* wooden bench used as a bed
271 *without* unless

260–1 *Come ... now* Carnochan suggests that the Shoemaker asks Dorimant for
money to drink his health: but 'next my heart' is used by Sir Frederick Frollick
when he embraces Jenny, Wheadle's maid (*Love in a Tub*, I.ii), and Brett-
Smith thinks the Shoemaker uses the phrase insolently.

271 *bloody drunk* the adverbial use of 'bloody' in colloquial language was recent, and
the *OED* cites this as its earliest example. However, the word appears in
Dryden's *The Wild Gallant*, I.i, 68–9, where Bibber, using tavern slang, says
'... I was drunk; damnably drunk with Ale; great Hogen Mogen bloody Ale; I
was porterly drunk ...' (*Works of John Dryden*, vol. 7, ed. J. H. Smith, D.
MacMillan, *et al*. (Berkeley and Los Angeles, 1962), p. 11). The modern usage
as a mere intensifier or as an adjective only dates from the nineteenth century.

SHOEMAKER

Tope's the word, i' the eye of the world. [*To* HANDY] For my master's honour, Robin!

DORIMANT

Do not debauch my servants, sirrah.

SHOEMAKER

I only tip him the wink; he knows an alehouse from a hovel.   275

Exit SHOEMAKER

DORIMANT [*to* HANDY]

My clothes, quickly!

MEDLEY

Where shall we dine today?

Enter YOUNG BELLAIR

DORIMANT

Where you will. Here comes a good third man.

YOUNG BELLAIR

Your servant, gentlemen.

MEDLEY

Gentle sir, how will you answer this visit to your honourable   280
mistress? 'Tis not her interest you should keep company with
men of sense, who will be talking reason.

YOUNG BELLAIR

I do not fear her pardon, do you but grant me yours for my
neglect of late.

272–3 *Tope's . . . Robin* CA (Q1, CO have no punctuation; Q2–3, B give a comma
after 'honour'; W, V give commas after 'world' and 'honour')
275 *tip . . . wink* give a private signal (orig. rogue's cant)

272–3 *Tope's . . . Robin.* Brett-Smith suggests that the Shoemaker rebukes Medley's vulgarism 'bloody drunk': 'tope' is the gentlemanly word. The
Shoemaker, with a wink at Handy, then performs the motions of drinking
Dorimant's health. 'Tope' was a relatively new word (*OED* cites its first
example from 1654), but was less recent than 'bloody'. But 'tope' may be used
as an exclamation, 'I pledge you' (from Fr. *tope*, to accept an offer or proposal,
or, in gambling, to cover a bet, accept a challenge): Palmer uses the word in
this sense in Etherege's *The Comical Revenge* (1664)—'Tope—here, pledg me'
(II.iii, 48). 'In that case, the Shoemaker accepts Medley's conditions, as (he
asserts) would the *world*' (Carnochan). This meaning would make the reading
of the early edd. possible though difficult. Some support may be given to this
by a recent emendation of Suckling's *The Goblins*, I.iv, 6 (*The Works of Sir John
Suckling*, ed. Thomas S. Clayton and Lester Beaurline (Oxford, 1971), vol. 2,
133)—'TAYLOR. Oh no! He seldome wears his Sword. SERGEANT. *Tope* is the
word if he do . . .' Suckling's play was written between 1637 and 1641, so that
this occurrence would precede the *OED*'s first example.

MEDLEY
  Though you've made us miserable by the want of your good   285
  company, to show you I am free from all resentment, may the
  beautiful cause of our misfortune give you all the joys happy
  lovers have shared ever since the world began.

YOUNG BELLAIR
  You wish me in heaven, but you believe me on my journey to
  hell.   290

MEDLEY
  You have a good strong faith, and that may contribute much
  towards your salvation. I confess I am but of an untoward
  constitution, apt to have doubts and scruples; and in love they
  are no less distracting than in religion. Were I so near marriage, I
  should cry out by fits as I ride in my coach, 'Cuckold, cuckold!'   295
  with no less fury than the mad fanatic does 'Glory!' in Bethlem.

YOUNG BELLAIR
  Because religion makes some run mad, must I live an atheist?

MEDLEY
  Is it not great indiscretion for a man of credit, who may have
  money enough on his word, to go and deal with Jews, who for
  little sums make men enter into bonds and give judgments?   300

YOUNG BELLAIR
  Preach no more on this text. I am determined, and there is no
  hope of my conversion.

DORIMANT (to HANDY, who is fiddling about him)
  Leave your unnecessary fiddling. A wasp that's buzzing about a
  man's nose at dinner is not more troublesome than thou art.

HANDY
  You love to have your clothes hang just, sir.   305

DORIMANT
  I love to be well-dressed, sir, and think it no scandal to my
  understanding.

---

292 *untoward* awkward, perverse
300 *judgments* judicial assignment of chattels, hence the certificate of such a judg-
    ment used as security

---

296 *mad fanatic ... Bethlem* Brett-Smith identifies as Oliver Cromwell's porter,
    Daniel, imprisoned in Bethlehem Hospital, the London lunatic asylum usually
    known as Bedlam. He cites the dialogue in 'A New Song of the Times, 1683'
    between 'Olivers Porter, Fidler, *and* Poet *In* BEDLAM' in which the porter
    begins, 'O Glory! Glory! who are these Appear?' (*A Second Collection of ...
    Poems ... against Popery* (1689), p. 12). There are other contemporary refer-
    ences: the Prologue to D'Urfey's *Sir Barnaby Whigg* (1681) has, 'Like *Lunaticks*
    ye roar ... Like Oliver's Porter, but not so devout'.

HANDY

Will you use the essence, or orange-flower water?

DORIMANT

I will smell as I do today, no offence to the ladies' noses.

HANDY

Your pleasure, sir.   [*Exit* HANDY] 310

DORIMANT

That a man's excellency should lie in neatly tying of a ribbon or a cravat! How careful's nature in furnishing the world with necessary coxcombs!

YOUNG BELLAIR

That's a mighty pretty suit of yours, Dorimant.

DORIMANT

I am glad 't has your approbation.   315

YOUNG BELLAIR

No man in town has a better fancy in his clothes than you have.

DORIMANT

You will make me have an opinion of my genius.

MEDLEY

There is a great critic, I hear, in these matters lately arrived piping hot from Paris.

YOUNG BELLAIR

Sir Fopling Flutter, you mean.   320

MEDLEY

The same.

YOUNG BELLAIR

He thinks himself the pattern of modern gallantry.

DORIMANT

He is indeed the pattern of modern foppery.

MEDLEY

He was yesterday at the play, with a pair of gloves up to his elbows and a periwig more exactly curled than a lady's head 325 newly dressed for a ball.

YOUNG BELLAIR

What a pretty lisp he has!

DORIMANT

Ho, that he affects in imitation of the people of quality of France.

MEDLEY

His head stands for the most part on one side, and his looks are

308 *essence* perfume, scent

---

308 *orange-flower water* see note to III.ii, 207.

316 *fancy* taste, critical judgment in matters of art or elegance. *OED* cites Mrs Hutchinson's *Memoirs of Colonel Hutchinson* (1665), p. 23, 'He was ... genteel in his habit [i.e., dress] and had a very good fancy in it'.

more languishing than a lady's when she lolls at stretch in her   330
coach or leans her head carelessly against the side of a box i' the
playhouse.

DORIMANT

He is a person indeed of great acquired follies.

MEDLEY

He is like many others, beholding to his education for making
him so eminent a coxcomb. Many a fool had been lost to the   335
world, had their indulgent parents wisely bestowed neither
learning nor good breeding on 'em.

YOUNG BELLAIR

He has been, as the sparkish word is, brisk upon the ladies
already. He was yesterday at my Aunt Townley's and gave Mrs
Loveit a catalogue of his good qualities under the character of a   340
complete gentleman, who (according to Sir Fopling) ought to
dress well, dance well, fence well, have a genius for love letters,
an agreeable voice for a chamber, be very amorous, something
discreet, but not over-constant.

MEDLEY

Pretty ingredients to make an accomplished person!   345

DORIMANT

I am glad he pitched upon Loveit.

YOUNG BELLAIR

How so?

DORIMANT

I wanted a fop to lay to her charge, and this is as pat as may be.

YOUNG BELLAIR

I am confident she loves no man but you.

DORIMANT

The good fortune were enough to make me vain, but that I am in   350
my nature modest.

YOUNG BELLAIR

Hark you, Dorimant.—With your leave, Mr Medley—'tis only a
secret concerning a fair lady.

MEDLEY

Your good breeding, sir, gives you too much trouble. You might
have whispered without all this ceremony.   355

YOUNG BELLAIR (to DORIMANT)

How stand your affairs with Bellinda of late?

334 *beholding* Q1 (beholden Q3)
338 *brisk* sharp

DORIMANT

She's a little jilting baggage.

YOUNG BELLAIR

Nay, I believe her false enough, but she's ne'er the worse for
your purpose. She was with you yesterday in a disguise at the
play.   360

DORIMANT

There we fell out and resolved never to speak to one another
more.

YOUNG BELLAIR

The occasion?

DORIMANT

Want of courage to meet me at the place appointed. These young
women apprehend loving as much as the young men do fighting   365
at first; but once entered, like them too, they all turn bullies
straight.

Enter HANDY

HANDY (*to* YOUNG BELLAIR)

Sir, your man without desires to speak with you.

YOUNG BELLAIR

Gentlemen, I'll return immediately.   *Exit* YOUNG BELLAIR

MEDLEY

A very pretty fellow, this.

DORIMANT   370

He's handsome, well-bred, and by much the most tolerable of all
the young men that do not abound in wit.

MEDLEY

Ever well-dressed, always complaisant, and seldom impertinent.
You and he are grown very intimate, I see.

DORIMANT

It is our mutual interest to be so. It makes the women think the
better of his understanding and judge more favourably of my   375
reputation; it makes him pass upon some for a man of very good
sense, and I upon others for a very civil person.

357 *baggage* used familiarly or playfully of any young woman (1672–   ), but the
    earlier meaning, a worthless good-for-nothing woman, a strumpet, remained
    current. *OED* cites W. Robertson, *Phraseologia Generalis* ... (1693 ed.), p.
    197, 'A baggage, or Souldier's Punk'.

366 *bullies* probably plays on different senses of the word—1) sweetheart (of either
    men or women), 2) blustering gallant, swashbuckler, 3) the 'gallant' or protec-
    tor of prostitutes.

373 *complaisant* obliging, courteous, accommodating. Cf. Hobbes, *Leviathan*, I.xv,
    76, 'Compleasance; that is to say, That every man strive to accomodate
    himselfe to the rest', and Johnson's *Dictionary*, 'Civility, desire of pleasing . . .'
    A recent word (first example in *OED* dated 1647). See Introduction, pp.
    xxxiii–iv.

MEDLEY
What was that whisper?

DORIMANT
A thing which he would fain have known, but I did not think it fit 380
to tell him. It might have frighted him from his honourable
intentions of marrying.

MEDLEY
Emilia, give her her due, has the best reputation of any young
woman about the town who has beauty enough to provoke
detraction. Her carriage is unaffected, her discourse mod- 385
est—not at all censorious nor pretending, like the counterfeits of
the age.

DORIMANT
She's a discreet maid, and I believe nothing can corrupt her but a
husband.

MEDLEY
A husband? 390

DORIMANT
Yes, a husband. I have known many women make a difficulty of
losing a maidenhead, who have afterwards made none of making
a cuckold.

MEDLEY
This prudent consideration, I am apt to think, has made you
confirm poor Bellair in the desperate resolution he has taken. 395

DORIMANT
Indeed, the little hope I found there was of her, in the state she
was in, has made me by my advice contribute something towards
the changing of her condition.

Enter YOUNG BELLAIR

Dear Bellair, by heavens I thought we had lost thee! Men in love
are never to be reckoned on when we would form a company. 400

YOUNG BELLAIR
Dorimant, I am undone. My man has brought the most surprising news i' the world.

DORIMANT
Some strange misfortune is befallen your love?

---

385 *carriage* either, deportment, or habitual manner of conduct

---

379–82 *that whisper ... marrying* the 'whisper' is the exchange between Young
Bellair and Dorimant (ll. 356–67), from which Medley has been excluded.
Thus, Dorimant first disguises his relationship with Bellinda from Young
Bellair (l. 357), so protecting her reputation (cf. IV.ii, 73–4), and then uses
Emilia as a blind when speaking to Medley.

YOUNG BELLAIR

My father came to town last night and lodges i' the very house where Emilia lies.

405

MEDLEY

Does he know it is with her you are in love?

YOUNG BELLAIR

He knows I love, but knows not whom, without some officious sot has betrayed me.

DORIMANT

Your Aunt Townley is your confidante and favours the business.

YOUNG BELLAIR

I do not apprehend any ill office from her. I have received a 410 letter, in which I am commanded by my father to meet him at my aunt's this afternoon. He tells me farther he has made a match for me, and bids me resolve to be obedient to his will or expect to be disinherited.

MEDLEY

Now's your time, Bellair. Never had lover such an opportunity 415 of giving a generous proof of his passion.

YOUNG BELLAIR

As how, I pray?

MEDLEY

Why, hang an estate, marry Emilia out of hand, and provoke your father to do what he threatens. 'Tis but despising a coach, humbling yourself to a pair of galoshes, being out of countenance 420 when you meet your friends, pointed at and pitied wherever you go by all the amorous fops that know you, and your fame will be immortal.

YOUNG BELLAIR

I could find in my heart to resolve not to marry at all.

DORIMANT

Fie, fie! That would spoil a good jest and disappoint the well- 425 natured town of an occasion of laughing at you.

YOUNG BELLAIR

The storm I have so long expected hangs o'er my head and begins to pour down upon me. I am on the rack and can have no rest till I'm satisfied in what I fear. Where do you dine?

---

420 *galoshes* CA (goloshoes Q1; goloshes V). '*Galloches*, high wooden Pattins or Clogs . . . It also means a Sort of Slipper worn over the Shoes' (Ozell's *Rabelais* (1737), vol. 2, 219: cited *OED*)

---

409 *confidante* this should perhaps be regarded as another instance of a French word. First instance, from Lady Mary Wortley Montagu, in *OED* dates from 1709. The word may have been formed to represent the sound of Fr. *confidente*.

DORIMANT
    At Long's or Locket's.   430
MEDLEY
    At Long's let it be.
YOUNG BELLAIR
    I'll run and see Emilia and inform myself how matters stand. If
    my misfortunes are not so great as to make me unfit for company,
    I'll be with you.   *Exit* YOUNG BELLAIR

                Enter a FOOTMAN *with a letter*

FOOTMAN (*to* DORIMANT)
    Here's a letter, sir.   435
DORIMANT
    The superscription's right: 'For Mr Dorimant'.
MEDLEY
    Let's see. [*Looks at the letter*] The very scrawl and spelling of a
    true-bred whore.
DORIMANT
    I know the hand. The style is admirable, I assure you.
MEDLEY
    Prithee, read it.   440
DORIMANT (*reads*)
    'I told a you you dud not love me, if you dud, you would have
    seen me again ere now. I have no money and am very malicolly.
    Pray send me a guynie to see the operies. Your servant to
    command, Molly'.
MEDLEY
    Pray let the whore have a favourable answer, that she may spark   445
    it in a box and do honour to her profession.
DORIMANT
    She shall, and perk up i' the face of quality. [*To* HANDY] Is the
    coach at door?
HANDY
    You did not bid me send for it.

---

430 *Long's or Locket's* well-known eating-places. There was a tavern called Long's
    in the Haymarket and another in Covent Garden, kept by two brothers.
    Locket's, named after its landlord, Adam Locket, is continually referred to in
    Restoration comedies, and was frequented by Etherege himself. Lord Fop-
    pington speaks of going 'to Dinner at *Lacket*'s; where you are so nicely and
    delicately serv'd, that, stap my Vitals, they shall compose you a Dish no bigger
    than a Saucer, shall come to Fifty shillings' (*The Relapse* (1697), II.i).
447 *perk up* assume or have a lively or self-conceited attitude or air; lift one's head,
    or thrust oneself forward briskly, boldly, or impudently. But possibly 'perk'
    (*OED*, V. 2), to perch, used of birds, though also transferred to people.

DORIMANT

Eternal blockhead! (HANDY *offers to go out*) Hey, sot!   450

HANDY

Did you call me, sir?

DORIMANT

I hope you have no just exception to the name, sir?

HANDY

I have sense, sir.

DORIMANT

Not so much as a fly in winter.—How did you come, Medley?

MEDLEY

In a chair.   455

FOOTMAN

You may have a hackney coach if you please, sir.

DORIMANT

I may ride the elephant if I please, sir. Call another chair and let
my coach follow to Long's.

'Be calm, ye great parents, etc.'

Exeunt, [DORIMANT] *singing*

457 *I . . . elephant* Professor Harold Brooks informs me that there are several
contemporary references to elephants exhibited in London from 1675 to 1682.
He kindly provides a citation from the *City Mercury*, No. 3, 11–18 Nov. 1675,
where an advertisement headed 'The Elephant' reads, 'That Wonderful Beast
lately sent from *East-India* to the Right Honourable *George Berkley*, And since
sold for Two thousand pounds sterling: Is now to be seen at the *White Horse*
Inn over against *Salisbury* Court in Fleet-Street . . .' (Further, see Professor
Brooks's D.Phil. on Oldham, Bodleian Library.)

459 *Be . . . parents, etc.* Conaghan identifies as from the song 'My Lord: Great
Neptune, for my Sake' in the final scene of Shadwell's operatic version of *The
Tempest* (1674). ll. 17–18 run: 'Be calm, ye great Parents of the Flouds and the
Springs, /While each *Nereide* and *Triton* Plays, Revels, and Sings' (*Complete
Works*, ed. M. Summers (1927), vol. 2, 266).

Act II, Scene i
[LADY TOWNLEY's *house*]

Enter my LADY TOWNLEY *and* EMILIA

LADY TOWNLEY
I was afraid, Emilia, all had been discovered.

EMILIA
I tremble with the apprehension still.

LADY TOWNLEY
That my brother should take lodgings i' the very house where
you lie!

EMILIA
'Twas lucky we had timely notice to warn the people to be secret.   5
He seems to be a mighty good-humoured old man.

LADY TOWNLEY
He ever had a notable smirking way with him.

EMILIA
He calls me rogue, tells me he can't abide me, and does so bepat
me.

LADY TOWNLEY
On my word, you are much in his favour then.   10

EMILIA
He has been very inquisitive, I am told, about my family, my
reputation, and my fortune.

LADY TOWNLEY
I am confident he does not i' the least suspect you are the woman
his son's in love with.

EMILIA
What should make him then inform himself so particularly of   15
me?

LADY TOWNLEY
He was always of a very loving temper himself. It may be he has a
doting fit upon him, who knows?

EMILIA
It cannot be.

Enter YOUNG BELLAIR

LADY TOWNLEY
Here comes my nephew.—Where did you leave your father?   20

YOUNG BELLAIR

Writing a note within. Emilia, this early visit looks as if some kind jealousy would not let you rest at home.

EMILIA

The knowledge I have of my rival gives me a little cause to fear your constancy.

YOUNG BELLAIR

My constancy! I vow—   25

EMILIA

Do not vow—our love is frail as is our life, and full as little in our power; and are you sure you shall outlive this day?

YOUNG BELLAIR

I am not, but when we are in perfect health, 'twere an idle thing to fright ourselves with the thoughts of sudden death.

LADY TOWNLEY

Pray, what has passed between you and your father i' the garden?   30

YOUNG BELLAIR

He's firm in his resolution, tells me I must marry Mrs Harriet, or swears he'll marry himself and disinherit me. When I saw I could not prevail with him to be more indulgent, I dissembled an obedience to his will, which has composed his passion and will give us time—and I hope opportunity—to deceive him.   35

Enter OLD BELLAIR *with a note in his hand*

LADY TOWNLEY

Peace, here he comes.

OLD BELLAIR

Harry, take this and let your man carry it for me to Mr Fourbe's chamber, my lawyer, i' the Temple.

[*Exit* YOUNG BELLAIR]

(*To* EMILIA) Neighbour, adod, I am glad to see thee here.—Make much of her, sister. She's one of the best of your   40 acquaintance. I like her countenance and her behaviour well; she has a modesty that is not common i' this age, adod she has.

LADY TOWNLEY

I know her value, brother, and esteem her accordingly.

---

37 *Fourbe's* Q1 varies spelling to 'Furb' at V.ii, 11, 28, but 'fourbe' (from the French) meant a cheat, an impostor, or a trick, imposture. A short-lived word: *OED* gives examples of the noun and verb from 1654 to 1761, and cites Denham's *Passion of Dido* (1668), l. 107, 'Thou art a false Impostor and a Fourbe'.

38 *Temple* the Inner and Middle Temple of London's Inns of Court are so-called because they stand on the site of the buildings of the Knights Templar.

OLD BELLAIR

Advise her to wear a little more mirth in her face. Adod, she's too
serious.   45

LADY TOWNLEY

The fault is very excusable in a young woman.

OLD BELLAIR

Nay, adod, I like her ne'er the worse; a melancholy beauty has
her charms. I love a pretty sadness in a face which varies now and
then, like changeable colours, into a smile.

LADY TOWNLEY

Methinks you speak very feelingly, brother.   50

OLD BELLAIR

I am but five-and-fifty, sister, you know—an age not altogether
insensible. (*To* EMILIA) Cheer up sweetheart, I have a secret to
tell thee may chance to make thee merry. We three will make
collation together anon. I' the meantime, mum! [*Aloud*] I can't
abide you; go, I can't abide you—   55

Enter YOUNG BELLAIR

Harry! Come, you must along with me to my Lady Woodvill's.—I am going to slip the boy at a mistress.

YOUNG BELLAIR

At a wife, sir, you would say.

OLD BELLAIR

You need not look so glum, sir. A wife is no curse when she
brings the blessing of a good estate with her. But an idle town   60
flirt, with a painted face, a rotten reputation, and a crazy fortune, adod, is the devil and all; and such a one I hear you are in
league with.

YOUNG BELLAIR

I cannot help detraction, sir.

---

47 *adod* equivalent to 'egad', 'By God'
54 *meantime . . . I* CA (meantime mum, I Q1; meantime, mum, I Q3). Conaghan
   cites two further contemporary texts for the emendation
57 *slip* release (a greyhound or hawk) from a leash or slip

---

54 *mum* two meanings are possible. 1) Hush, be silent! (the meaning assumed by
   this text). 2) A vulgar variant of 'madam'.
61 *flirt* woman of loose character (1600–1703, *OED*, which cites this e.g.). The
   first example of the modern sense (one who flirts or plays at courtship) given by
   the *OED* is from Richardson in 1748.

OLD BELLAIR

Out a pize o' their breeches, there are keeping fools enough for 65
such flaunting baggages, and they are e'en too good for 'em. (*To*
EMILIA) Remember 'night. [*Aloud*] Go, you're a rogue, you're a
rogue. Fare you well, fare you well. [*To* YOUNG BELLAIR] Come,
come, come along, sir.

Exeunt OLD *and* YOUNG BELLAIR

LADY TOWNLEY

On my word, the old man comes on apace. I'll lay my life he's 70
smitten.

EMILIA

This is nothing but the pleasantness of his humour.

LADY TOWNLEY

I know him better than you. Let it work; it may prove lucky.

Enter a PAGE

PAGE

Madam, Mr Medley has sent to know whether a visit will not be
troublesome this afternoon?

LADY TOWNLEY 75

Send him word his visits never are so.   [*Exit* PAGE]

EMILIA

He's a very pleasant man.

LADY TOWNLEY

He's a very necessary man among us women. He's not scandalous i' the least, perpetually contriving to bring good company
together, and always ready to stop up a gap at ombre. Then, he 80
knows all the little news o' the town.

EMILIA

I love to hear him talk o' the intrigues. Let 'em be never so dull in
themselves, he'll make 'em pleasant i' the relation.

---

65 *keeping fools* fools who keep mistresses (cf. Dryden's title, *Mr Limberham, or,
The Kind Keeper*)

---

65 *pize* imprecation of uncertain meaning. It may be an arbitrary substitute for
'Pest!' or 'Pox!', the latter being used in the same way as 'pize' from 1600
onwards.

66 *baggages* see note to I, 357.

80, 92 *ombre* a card-game, fashionable in the seventeenth and early eighteenth
centuries. Played by three people, with forty cards, the eights, nines, and tens
of the ordinary pack being thrown out. A Spanish game according to Cotgrave,
so-called because 'he who undertakes to play [for the stake] saith *Yo soy
L'Ombre*, i.e., I am the man . . .' Matadore (l. 101) was the name given to the
principal cards (the black aces and variable card).

LADY TOWNLEY
But he improves things so much one can take no measure of the
truth from him. Mr Dorimant swears a flea or a maggot is not   85
made more monstrous by a magnifying glass than a story is by his
telling it.

Enter MEDLEY

EMILIA
Hold, here he comes.
LADY TOWNLEY
Mr Medley.
MEDLEY
Your servant, madam.   90
LADY TOWNLEY
You have made yourself a stranger of late.
EMILIA
I believe you took a surfeit of ombre last time you were here.
MEDLEY
Indeed I had my bellyful of that termagant, Lady Dealer. There
was so insatiable a carder; an old gleeker never loved to sit
to 't like her. I have played with her now at least a dozen times, 95
till she's worn out all her fine complexion and her tour would
keep in curl no longer.
LADY TOWNLEY
Blame her not, poor woman. She loves nothing so well as a black
ace.
MEDLEY
The pleasure I have seen her in when she has had hope in   100
drawing for a matadore!
EMILIA
'Tis as pretty sport to her as persuading masks off is to you, to
make discoveries.
LADY TOWNLEY
Pray, where's your friend Mr Dorimant?

---

94 *carder* card-player (obs.: *OED* gives examples *c.* 1530–1712)

---

94 *gleeker* player of gleek, a card-game (rare). The game was played by three
people; forty-four cards were used, twelve being dealt to each player, the
remaining eight forming a common 'stock'.
96 *tour* a crescent of false hair. Another word of French extraction (cf. *tour de
cheveux*) newly brought into English (*OED* gives first e.g. from 1674). Cham-
bers's *Cyclopaedia* (1724–41) describes as 'a tress or border of hair, going round
the head, which mingled dextrously with the natural hair, lengthens and
thickens it'.

MEDLEY

Soliciting his affairs. He's a man of great employment—has   105
more mistresses now depending than the most eminent lawyer in
England has causes.

EMILIA

Here has been Mrs Loveit so uneasy and out of humour these
two days.

LADY TOWNLEY

How strangely love and jealousy rage in that poor woman!   110

MEDLEY

She could not have picked out a devil upon earth so proper to
torment her. He's made her break a dozen or two of fans already,
tear half a score points in pieces, and destroy hoods and knots
without number.

LADY TOWNLEY

We heard of a pleasant serenade he gave her t'other night.   115

MEDLEY

A Danish serenade, with kettledrums and trumpets.

EMILIA

Oh, barbarous!

MEDLEY

What, you are of the number of the ladies whose ears are grown

---

106 *depending* pending, like a lawyer's cases (causes)
112 *He's* ed. (Has Q1; h'as Q3, B, CO; H'as CA; he has W, V)
113 *points* pieces of tagged lace or cord for fastening clothes
113 *knots* bows made of ribbon

115, 116 *serenade . . . Danish serenade* 'serenade' was a recent word from the French
(first e.g. in *OED* is from 1649). Medley indicates that French wind instruments were an expected part of the ensemble (ll. 119–20), as they are of Sir
Fopling's *equipage* (see IV.i, 253). Dorimant's 'Danish serenade' is a drunken
practical joke. Carnochan aptly cites *Hamlet*, I.iv, 8–12, 'The King doth wake
tonight and takes his rouse, /Keeps wassail, and the swaggering upspring reels';
/And as he drains his draughts of Rhenish down, /The kettledrum and trumpet
thus bray out /The triumph of his pledge'.

so delicate since our operas, you can be charmed with nothing
but flutes douces and French hautboys?   120

EMILIA

Leave your raillery and tell us, is there any new wit come
forth—songs, or novels?

MEDLEY

A very pretty piece of gallantry, by an eminent author, called *The
Diversions of Brussels*—very necessary to be read by all old ladies
who are desirous to improve themselves at questions and com-   125
mands, blindman's buff, and the like fashionable recreations.

EMILIA

Oh, ridiculous!

MEDLEY

Then there is *The Art of Affectation*, written by a late beauty of
quality, teaching you how to draw up your breasts, stretch up
your neck, to thrust out your breech, to play with your head, to   130
toss up your nose, to bite your lips, to turn up your eyes, to speak
in a silly soft tone of a voice, and use all the foolish French words

---

120 *flutes douces* ed. (Flute doux Q1; *flûtes douces* V, CA)

---

119 *operas* the production of the altered versions of *Macbeth* (1673) and *The Tempest*
(1674) along with Shadwell's *Psyche* (1675), all of them elaborate spectacles
which had musical elements, marked a new stage in the development of
Restoration 'opera'. Brett-Smith cites Evelyn's *Diary*, 5 Jan. 1673/74, 'I saw an
Italian opera in musiq, the first that had been seen of this kind'.

120 *flutes douces* Q1's 'doux' is an erroneous formation from the French. The flute
douce (i.e., the recorder) with its eight holes and two octaves succeeded the
flageolet (see note to III.iii, 228) in popularity, but was a recent introduction to
England. Evelyn's *Diary*, 20 Nov. 1679, records, 'There was also a flute douce,
now much in request for accompanying the voice'.

121 *raillery* imported from the French. First recorded instance in *OED* dates from
1653—'The word Raillery you return'd me for interpretation . . . is now grown
here so common with the better sort, as there are few of the meaner that are not
able to construe it' (R. Loveday, *Letters* (1663), p. 245).

123-4 *The Diversions of Brussels* identified by R. S. Cox as Richard Flecknoe's *A
Treatise of the Sports of Wit* (1675). See 'Richard Flecknoe and *The Man of
Mode*', *Modern Language Quarterly*, vol. 29 (1968), 183–9.

125-6 *questions and commands* a game in which one person addressed ludicrous
questions and commands to each member of the company. The game is seen as
similarly unfashionable in Wycherley's *Gentleman Dancing-Master* (1673), 'He
is as dull as a country-squire at questions and commands' (II.ii).

128 *The Art of Affectation* Medley is mocking Hannah Woolley's *The Gentlewoman's
Companion* (1675). Conaghan notes that the book advises the raising of the eyes
heavenwards ('Of the Government of the Eye', p. 39) and refers to washing and
painting as 'innocently helpful to the beauties of modest women' (p. 240).
Medley's attribution to 'a late beauty of quality' may be based on the portrait at
the front of the book.

that will infallibly make your person and conversation charming;
with a short apology at the latter end, in the behalf of young
ladies who notoriously wash and paint, though they have natur-   135
ally good complexions.

EMILIA
What a deal of stuff you tell us!

MEDLEY
Such as the town affords, madam. The Russians, hearing the
great respect we have for foreign dancing, have lately sent over
some of their best baladines, who are now practising a famous   140
ballet which will be suddenly danced at the Bear Garden.

LADY TOWNLEY
Pray forbear your idle stories, and give us an account of the state
of love as it now stands.

MEDLEY
Truly, there has been some revolutions in those affairs—great
chopping and changing among the old and some new lovers,   145
whom malice, indiscretion, and misfortune have luckily brought
into play.

LADY TOWNLEY
What think you of walking into the next room and sitting down,
before you engage in this business?

MEDLEY
I wait upon you; and I hope (though women are commonly   150
unreasonable), by the plenty of scandal I shall discover, to give
you very good content, ladies.   *Exeunt*

---

135 *wash* use cosmetic washes
141 *suddenly* soon

---

140 *baladine* a theatrical dancer; a mountebank, buffoon (from the French). This
occurrence is the *OED*'s first clear example of the word being restricted to
dancers, though it occurs as early as 1599.
141 *ballet* originally employed to illustrate dramatically the costumes and manners
of other nations. A new word from the French: the only earlier occurrence in
the *OED* is from Dryden's *Essay of Dramatick Poesie* (1667).
141 *Bear Garden* a hit both at the contemporary craze for music and dancing by
foreign troupes, and at the proverbial barbarity of the Russians—the Bear
Garden, on Bankside, was a venue for bear-baiting and prizefighting with
swords. (Perhaps the bears there danced?)
145 *chopping and changing* the phrase originally meant buying and selling, barter-
ing. As Carnochan observes, the words keep something of that force here.

Act II, Scene ii
[MRS LOVEIT's]

Enter MRS LOVEIT *and* PERT. MRS LOVEIT *putting up a letter, then pulling out her pocket-glass and looking in it*

MRS LOVEIT
Pert.

PERT
Madam?

MRS LOVEIT
I hate myself, I look so ill today.

PERT
Hate the wicked cause on't, that base man, Mr Dorimant, who   5
makes you torment and vex yourself continually.

MRS LOVEIT
He is to blame, indeed.

PERT
To blame to be two days without sending, writing, or coming
near you, contrary to his oath and covenant! 'Twas to much
purpose to make him swear! I'll lay my life there's not an article   10
but he has broken—talked to the vizards i' the pit, waited upon
the ladies from the boxes to their coaches, gone behind the
scenes and fawned upon those little insignificant creatures, the
players. 'Tis impossible for a man of his inconstant temper to
forbear, I'm sure.

MRS LOVEIT
I know he is a devil, but he has something of the angel yet   15
undefaced in him, which makes him so charming and agreeable
that I must love him, be he never so wicked.

PERT
I little thought, madam, to see your spirit tamed to this degree,
who banished poor Mr Lackwit but for taking up another lady's
fan in your presence.   20

MRS LOVEIT
My knowing of such odious fools contributes to the making of me
love Dorimant the better.

PERT
Your knowing of Mr Dorimant, in my mind, should rather make
you hate all mankind.

MRS LOVEIT
So it does, besides himself.   25

1 s.d. *putting up* putting away

PERT

Pray, what excuse does he make in his letter?

MRS LOVEIT

He has had business.

PERT

Business in general terms would not have been a current excuse
for another. A modish man is always very busy when he is in
pursuit of a new mistress.   30

MRS LOVEIT

Some fop has bribed you to rail at him. He had business; I will
believe it, and will forgive him.

PERT

You may forgive him anything, but I shall never forgive him his
turning me into ridicule, as I hear he does.

MRS LOVEIT

I perceive you are of the number of those fools his wit has made   35
his enemies.

PERT

I am of the number of those he's pleased to rally, madam; and if
we may believe Mr Wagfan and Mr Caperwell, he sometimes
makes merry with yourself, too, among his laughing compan-
ions.   40

MRS LOVEIT

Blockheads are as malicious to witty men as ugly women are to
the handsome; 'tis their interest, and they make it their business
to defame 'em.

PERT

I wish Mr Dorimant would not make it his business to defame
you.   45

MRS LOVEIT

Should he, I had rather be made infamous by him than owe my
reputation to the dull discretion of those fops you talk of.

Enter BELLINDA

Bellinda!   *Running to her*

BELLINDA

My dear!

MRS LOVEIT

You have been unkind of late.   50

28 *current* genuine
35 *has* W, V, B, CA (had Q1)
47 *of* Q3, V, B, CA (off Q1)

29 *modish* from the French, *mode*, a recent importation. First example in *OED*
dates from 1660.

BELLINDA

Do not say unkind, say unhappy.

MRS LOVEIT

I could chide you. Where have you been these two days?

BELLINDA

Pity me rather, my dear, where I have been so tired with two or three country gentlewomen, whose conversation has been more insufferable than a country fiddle. 55

MRS LOVEIT

Are they relations?

BELLINDA

No, Welsh acquaintance I made when I was last year at St Winifred's. They have asked me a thousand questions of the modes and intrigues of the town, and I have told 'em almost as many things for news that hardly were so when their gowns were 60 in fashion.

MRS LOVEIT

Provoking creatures, how could you endure 'em?

BELLINDA (aside)

Now to carry on my plot; nothing but love could make me capable of so much falsehood. 'Tis time to begin, lest Dorimant should come before her jealousy has stung her. 65

(Laughs, and then speaks on)

I was yesterday at a play with 'em, where I was fain to show 'em the living, as the man at Westminster does the dead. That is Mrs Such-a-one, admired for her beauty; this is Mr Such-a-one, cried up for a wit; that is sparkish Mr Such-a-one, who keeps reverend Mrs Such-a-one; and there sits fine Mrs Such-a-one, 70 who was lately cast off by my Lord Such-a-one.

MRS LOVEIT

Did you see Dorimant there?

BELLINDA

I did, and imagine you were there with him and have no mind to own it.

59 *intrigues* liaisons, recently imported from the French. *OED* cites Charleton, *Ephesian and Cimmerian Matrons* (1668), 'She in like manner falls into an Intrigue (as they nowadays call it)'. Also Dryden, *Marriage à-la-Mode* (1673), 'Intrigue, Philotis! that's an old phrase; I have laid that word by; amour sounds better' (II.i).

67 *man at Westminster* a guide at Westminster Abbey. Conaghan cites Walter Pope, 'It is a Custom for the Servants of the Church upon all Holidays, *Sundays* excepted, betwixt the Sermon and Evening Prayers, to shew the Tombs, and Effigies of the Kings and Queens in Wax, to the meaner sort of People, who then flock thither from all the corners of the Town, and pay their Twopence to see *The Play of the Dead Volks*, as I have heard a *Devonshire* Clown not improperly call it' (*The Life of Seth Lord Bishop of Salisbury* (1697), p. 157).

MRS LOVEIT
What should make you think so?   75
BELLINDA
A lady masked, in a pretty dishabille, whom Dorimant enter-
tained with more respect than the gallants do a common vizard.
MRS LOVEIT (*aside*)
Dorimant at the play entertaining a mask! Oh, heavens!
BELLINDA (*aside*)
Good!
MRS LOVEIT
Did he stay all the while?   80
BELLINDA
Till the play was done, and then led her out, which confirms me
it was you.
MRS LOVEIT
Traitor!
PERT
Now you may believe he had business, and you may forgive him
too.   85
MRS LOVEIT
Ungrateful, perjured man!
BELLINDA
You seem so much concerned, my dear, I fear I have told you
unawares what I had better have concealed for your quiet.
MRS LOVEIT
What manner of shape had she?
BELLINDA
Tall and slender. Her motions were very genteel. Certainly she   90
must be some person of condition.
MRS LOVEIT
Shame and confusion be ever in her face when she shows it!
BELLINDA
I should blame your discretion for loving that wild man, my

76 *dishabille* ed. (dishabillié Q1; *déshabillé* V, CA)
90 *genteel* graceful, elegant

---

76 *in ... dishabille* a dress of negligent style. Wycherley's *Gentleman Dancing-
Master* (1673) has 'her dishabillie, or flame-colour gown called Indian' (V.i).
Another word newly taken over from the French: the spellings in Wycherley
and Q1 indicate that the word was in the process of being naturalized, though
there is no need to give as French as do Verity and Carnochan.
93 *wild man* possibly a reference to the traditional figure of the wild or 'salvage'
man (Q1 capitalizes 'wild': both words are capitalized in *Works* (1704)). On the
range of meanings of 'wild' in the play see Introduction, pp. xxix–xxxi.

dear—but they say he has a way so bewitching that few can
defend their hearts who know him.   95

MRS LOVEIT

I will tear him from mine, or die i' the attempt!

BELLINDA

Be more moderate.

MRS LOVEIT

Would I had daggers, darts, or poisoned arrows in my breast, so
I could but remove the thoughts of him from thence!

BELLINDA

Fie, fie, your transports are too violent, my dear. This may be   100
but an accidental gallantry, and 'tis likely ended at her coach.

PERT

Should it proceed farther, let your comfort be, the conduct Mr
Dorimant affects will quickly make you know your rival—ten to
one let you see her ruined, her reputation exposed to the
town—a happiness none will envy her but yourself, madam.   105

MRS LOVEIT

Whoe'er she be, all the harm I wish her is, may she love him as
well as I do, and may he give her as much cause to hate him!

PERT

Never doubt the latter end of your curse, madam!

MRS LOVEIT

May all the passions that are raised by neglected love—jealousy,
indignation, spite, and thirst of revenge—eternally rage in her   110
soul, as they do now in mine!

Walks up and down with a distracted air

Enter a PAGE

PAGE

Madam, Mr Dorimant—

MRS LOVEIT

I will not see him.

PAGE

I told him you were within, madam.

MRS LOVEIT

Say you lied, say I'm busy, shut the door—say anything!   115

PAGE

He's here, madam.   [*Exit* PAGE]

Enter DORIMANT

DORIMANT

'They taste of death who do at heaven arrive,
But we this paradise approach alive'.

117–18 *They ... alive* from Waller's 'Of her Chamber', ll. 1–2 (*Poems*, ed. G.
Thorn Drury (1901), vol. 1, 26). Dorimant has 'who' for Waller's 'that'.

(*To* MRS LOVEIT) What, dancing the galloping nag without a
fiddle? (*Offers to catch her by the hand; she flings away and walks*   120
on) I fear this restlessness of the body, madam, (*pursuing her*)
proceeds from an unquietness of the mind. What unlucky acci-
dent puts you out of humour—a point ill-washed, knots spoiled
i' the making up, hair shaded awry, or some other little mistake
in setting you in order?   125

PERT

A trifle, in my opinion, sir, more inconsiderable than any you
mention.

DORIMANT

Oh, Mrs Pert! I never knew you sullen enough to be silent.
Come, let me know the business.

PERT

The business, sir, is the business that has taken you up these two   130
days. How have I seen you laugh at men of business, and now to
become a man of business yourself!

DORIMANT

We are not masters of our own affections; our inclinations daily
alter. Now we love pleasure, and anon we shall dote on business.
Human frailty will have it so, and who can help it?   135

MRS LOVEIT

Faithless, inhuman, barbarous man—

DORIMANT [*aside*]

Good. Now the alarm strikes—

MRS LOVEIT

—Without sense of love, of honour, or of gratitude! Tell me, for
I will know, what devil masked she was, you were with at the
play yesterday.   140

DORIMANT

Faith, I resolved as much as you, but the devil was obstinate and
would not tell me.

MRS LOVEIT

False in this as in your vows to me! You do know!

DORIMANT

The truth is, I did all I could to know.

MRS LOVEIT

And dare you own it to my face? Hell and furies!   145

Tears her fan in pieces

DORIMANT

Spare your fan, madam. You are growing hot and will want it to
cool you.

---

119 *galloping nag* country dance, according to Carnochan.

MRS LOVEIT
   Horror and distraction seize you, sorrow and remorse gnaw your
   soul, and punish all your perjuries to me!   *Weeps*

DORIMANT (*turning to* BELLINDA)
         'So thunder breaks the cloud in twain,   150
            And makes a passage for the rain'.
   (*To* BELLINDA) Bellinda, you are the devil that have raised this
   storm. You were at the play yesterday and have been making
   discoveries to your dear.

BELLINDA
   You're the most mistaken man i' the world.   155

DORIMANT
   It must be so, and here I vow revenge—resolve to pursue and
   persecute you more impertinently than ever any loving fop did
   his mistress, hunt you i' the Park, trace you i' the Mall, dog you
   in every visit you make, haunt you at the plays and i' the drawing
   room, hang my nose in your neck and talk to you whether you   160
   will or no, and ever look upon you with such dying eyes till your
   friends grow jealous of me, send you out of town, and the world
   suspect your reputation. (*In a lower voice*)—At my Lady Townley's when we go from hence—   *He looks kindly on* BELLINDA

BELLINDA
   —I'll meet you there.   165

DORIMANT
   Enough.

MRS LOVEIT (*pushing* DORIMANT *away*)
   Stand off! You shan't stare upon her so!

DORIMANT [*aside*]
   Good! There's one made jealous already.

MRS LOVEIT
   Is this the constancy you vowed?

150–1 *So ... rain* from Matthew Roydon's 'An Elegie, or friend's passion for his
      Astrophill', ll. 59–60: identified by R. G. Howarth, 'Untraced Quotations in
      Etherege', *N & Q*, vol. 188 (June 1945), 281. Dorimant has 'breaks' for the
      original's 'rends'. Roydon's elegy for Sir Philip Sidney was published in *The
      Phoenix Nest* (1593).
158 *Park* either Hyde Park or St James's Park, which were both fashionable
      meeting-places, but probably the latter.
158 *the Mall* a broad avenue with four lines of trees laid out on the border of St
      James's Park by Charles II as a place to play pall mall (hence the name). Q1
      regularly spells 'Mail', reflecting the French origin of 'mall' (avenue, mallet
      used in the game). It is likely that Etherege intended the French pronuncia-
      tion: cf. Blount's *Glossographia* (1656), '*Pale Maille*, This game was heretofore
      used at the Alley near St Jameses, and vulgarly called Pel-Mel'.

DORIMANT

Constancy at my years? 'Tis not a virtue in season; you might as   170
well expect the fruit the autumn ripens i' the spring.

MRS LOVEIT

Monstrous principle!

DORIMANT

Youth has a long journey to go, madam. Should I have set up my
rest at the first inn I lodged at, I should never have arrived at the
happiness I now enjoy.   175

MRS LOVEIT

Dissembler, damned dissembler!

DORIMANT

I am so, I confess. Good nature and good manners corrupt me. I
am honest in my inclinations and would not, wer't not to avoid
offence, make a lady a little in years believe I think her young,
wilfully mistake art for nature, and seem as fond of a thing I am   180
weary of as when I doted on't in earnest.

MRS LOVEIT

False man!

DORIMANT

True woman.

MRS LOVEIT

Now you begin to show yourself!

DORIMANT

Love gilds us over and makes us show fine things to one another   185
for a time, but soon the gold wears off, and then again the native
brass appears.

MRS LOVEIT

Think on your oaths, your vows, and protestations, perjured
man!

DORIMANT

I made 'em when I was in love.   190

MRS LOVEIT

And therefore ought they not to bind? Oh, impious!

DORIMANT

What we swear at such a time may be a certain proof of a present
passion; but to say truth, in love there is no security to be given
for the future.

MRS LOVEIT

Horrid and ungrateful, begone! And never see me more!   195

174 *rest* abode
181 *of as* Q2–3, V, B, CA (off as Q1)

DORIMANT

I am not one of those troublesome coxcombs who, because they were once well-received, take the privilege to plague a woman with their love ever after. I shall obey you, madam, though I do myself some violence.

He offers to go, and MRS LOVEIT *pulls him back*

MRS LOVEIT

Come back, you shan't go! Could you have the ill nature to offer   200
it?

DORIMANT

When love grows diseased, the best thing we can do is to put it to a violent death. I cannot endure the torture of a lingering and consumptive passion.

MRS LOVEIT

Can you think mine sickly?   205

DORIMANT

Oh, 'tis desperately ill! What worse symptoms are there than your being always uneasy when I visit you, your picking quarrels with me on slight occasions, and in my absence kindly listening to the impertinences of every fashionable fool that talks to you?

MRS LOVEIT

What fashionable fool can you lay to my charge?   210

DORIMANT

Why, the very cock-fool of all those fools, Sir Fopling Flutter.

MRS LOVEIT

I never saw him in my life but once.

DORIMANT

The worse woman you, at first sight to put on all your charms, to entertain him with that softness in your voice and all that wanton kindness in your eyes you so notoriously affect when you design a   215
conquest.

MRS LOVEIT

So damned a lie did never malice yet invent. Who told you this?

DORIMANT

No matter. That ever I should love a woman that can dote on a senseless caper, a tawdry French ribbon, and a formal cravat.

MRS LOVEIT

You make me mad!   220

DORIMANT

A guilty conscience may do much! Go on, be the game-mistress of the town and enter all our young fops, as fast as they come from travel.

MRS LOVEIT

Base and scurrilous!

211 *cock-fool* a nonce formation

DORIMANT

A fine mortifying reputation 'twill be for a woman of your pride,   225
wit, and quality!

MRS LOVEIT

This jealousy's a mere pretence, a cursed trick of your own
devising. I know you.

DORIMANT

Believe it and all the ill of me you can. I would not have a woman
have the least good thought of me that can think well of Fopling.   230
Farewell. Fall to, and much good may do you with your coxcomb.

MRS LOVEIT

Stay! Oh stay, and I will tell you all.

DORIMANT

I have been told too much already.   *Exit* DORIMANT

MRS LOVEIT

Call him again!   235

PERT

E'en let him go. A fair riddance!

MRS LOVEIT

Run, I say! Call him again, I will have him called!

PERT

The devil should carry him away first, were it my concern.

                                         Exit PERT

BELLINDA

He's frighted me from the very thoughts of loving men. For
heaven's sake, my dear, do not discover what I told you. I dread   240
his tongue as much as you ought to have done his friendship.

Enter PERT

PERT

He's gone, madam.

MRS LOVEIT

Lightning blast him!

PERT

When I told him you desired him to come back, he smiled, made
a mouth at me, flung into his coach, and said—   245

MRS LOVEIT

What did he say?

231 *to* Q2–3, W, V, CA (too Q1)   231 *may* Q1 (may [it] V)

---

231 *much good may do you* a conventional ironic formula. Brett-Smith cites Ravens-
croft's *London Cuckolds* (1682), I.i: '*Wiseacre.* You have a witty wife, much
good may doe you with her./ *Doodle.* And much good may doe you with your
fool'. There is no need for Verity's emendation.

PERT

'Drive away'—and then repeated verses.

MRS LOVEIT

Would I had made a contract to be a witch when first I entertained this greater devil. Monster, barbarian! I could tear myself
in pieces. Revenge, nothing but revenge can ease me. Plague,   250
war, famine, fire—all that can bring universal ruin and misery
on mankind—with joy I'd perish to have you in my power but
this moment!

Exit MRS LOVEIT

PERT

Follow, madam. Leave her not in this outrageous passion.

PERT *gathers up the things*

BELLINDA

He's given me the proof which I desired of his love, but 'tis a   255
proof of his ill nature too. I wish I had not seen him use her so:

I sigh to think that Dorimant may be

One day as faithless and unkind to me.   *Exeunt*

Act III, Scene i
LADY WOODVILL's *lodgings*

Enter HARRIET *and* BUSY, *her woman*

BUSY
Dear madam! Let me set that curl in order.

HARRIET
Let me alone. I will shake 'em all out of order!

BUSY
Will you never leave this wildness?

HARRIET
Torment me not.

BUSY
Look! There's a knot falling off.   5

HARRIET
Let it drop.

BUSY
But one pin, dear madam.

HARRIET
How do I daily suffer under thy officious fingers!

BUSY
Ah, the difference that is between you and my Lady Dapper!
How uneasy she is if the least thing be amiss about her!   10

HARRIET
She is indeed most exact. Nothing is ever wanting to make her
ugliness remarkable.

BUSY
Jeering people say so.

HARRIET
Her powdering, painting, and her patching never fail in public to
draw the tongues and eyes of all the men upon her.   15

BUSY
She is indeed a little too pretending.

HARRIET
That women should set up for beauty as much in spite of nature
as some men have done for wit!

5 *knot* decorative ribbon

---

3 *wildness* restiveness. On 'wild' see Introduction pp. xxix–xxxi.
14 *patching* it was fashionable for women to wear small patches, normally of black
silk, on the face.

BUSY

    I hope without offence one may endeavour to make one's self
agreeable.   20

HARRIET

    Not when 'tis impossible. Women then ought to be no more fond
of dressing than fools should be of talking. Hoods and modesty,
masks and silence, things that shadow and conceal—they should
think of nothing else.

BUSY

    Jesu! Madam, what will your mother think is become of you?   25
For heaven's sake, go in again.

HARRIET

    I won't.

BUSY

    This is the extravagant'st thing that ever you did in your life, to
leave her and a gentleman who is to be your husband.

HARRIET

    My husband! Hast thou so little wit to think I spoke what I   30
meant when I overjoyed her in the country with a low curtsy and
'What you please, madam; I shall ever be obedient'?

BUSY

    Nay, I know not, you have so many fetches.

HARRIET

    And this was one, to get her up to London. Nothing else, I assure
thee.   35

BUSY

    Well, the man, in my mind, is a fine man!

HARRIET

    The man indeed wears his clothes fashionably and has a pretty,
negligent way with him, very courtly and much affected. He
bows, and talks, and smiles so agreeably, as he thinks.

BUSY

    I never saw anything so genteel.   40

HARRIET

    Varnished over with good breeding many a blockhead makes a
tolerable show.

BUSY

    I wonder you do not like him.

HARRIET

    I think I might be brought to endure him, and that is all a

---

33 *fetches* dodges, tricks

28 *extravagant'st* see Introduction, pp. xxxi–iii.

reasonable woman should expect in a husband; but there is duty   45
i' the case, and like the haughty Merab, I
        'Find much aversion in my stubborn mind',
which
        'Is bred by being promised and designed'.

BUSY

I wish you do not design your own ruin! I partly guess your   50
inclinations, madam. That Mr Dorimant—

HARRIET

Leave your prating and sing some foolish song or other.

BUSY

I will—the song you love so well ever since you saw Mr Dorimant.

SONG

When first Amintas charmed my heart,   55
My heedless sheep began to stray;
The wolves soon stole the greatest part,
And all will now be made a prey.

Ah, let not love your thoughts possess,
'Tis fatal to a shepherdess;   60
The dang'rous passion you must shun,
Or else like me be quite undone.

HARRIET

Shall I be paid down by a covetous parent for a purchase? I need
no land. No, I'll lay myself out all in love. It is decreed—

Enter YOUNG BELLAIR

YOUNG BELLAIR

What generous resolution are you making, madam?   65

HARRIET

Only to be disobedient, sir.

48 *which* B, CA, CO (omitted Q1, V; Q2–3, W include 'Which' but place it at the
beginning of the couplet, 'Which is ... designed'; in Q1 'which' is given as a
catchword on p. 32, and is clearly meant to link the two quotations)
64 *lay ... out* spend myself

46–49 *Merab ... designed* Merab, elder daughter of Saul, who should have been
given to David, but was married to Adriel (I Samuel 18.19). Harriet adapts
Abraham Cowley's description in *Davideis* (1656), Book III: 'And much
aversion in her stubborn mind /Was bred by being *promis'd* and *design'd*'
(*Poems*, ed. A. R. Waller (1905), p. 341).
55–62 SONG often reprinted; see Thorpe, p. 102, who also points out that Amintas
has something of the charm and dangerousness of Dorimant. For Dr Staggins's
setting, published in 1684, see Appendix A.

YOUNG BELLAIR
Let me join hands with you in that.

HARRIET
With all my heart. I never thought I should have given you mine
so willingly. Here, [*they join hands*]—I, Harriet—

YOUNG BELLAIR
And I, Harry—   70

HARRIET
Do solemnly protest—

YOUNG BELLAIR
And vow—

HARRIET
That I with you—

YOUNG BELLAIR
And I with you—

HARRIET, YOUNG BELLAIR
Will never marry.   75

HARRIET
A match!

YOUNG BELLAIR
And no match! How do you like this indifference now?

HARRIET
You expect I should take it ill, I see.

YOUNG BELLAIR
'Tis not unnatural for you women to be a little angry you miss a
conquest—though you would slight the poor man were he in   80
your power.

HARRIET
There are some, it may be, have an eye like Bart'lomew, big
enough for the whole fair, but I am not of the number, and you
may keep your gingerbread. 'Twill be more acceptable to the
lady whose dear image it wears, sir.   85

YOUNG BELLAIR
I must confess, madam, you came a day after the fair.

HARRIET
You own then you are in love?

79 *for you* Q1 (for young Q2–3)
86 *you . . . fair* too late (proverbial)

82–3 *an eye . . . fair* an allusion to Cokes in Jonson's *Bartholmew Fair* (1614), Act
III. The fair was held annually on 24 August in Smithfield.
84 *gingerbread* from 'gingimbrat' (M.E.), preserved ginger. The final syllable was
early confounded with 'bread', and gingerbread, made into various shapes and
often gilded, was a staple item at fairs. From 1605 the word also carried the
figurative meaning, 'anything showy and unsubstantial'.

YOUNG BELLAIR

    I do.

HARRIET

    The confidence is generous, and in return I could almost find in
my heart to let you know my inclinations.   90

YOUNG BELLAIR

    Are you in love?

HARRIET

    Yes—with this dear town, to that degree I can scarce endure the
country in landscapes and in hangings.

YOUNG BELLAIR

    What a dreadful thing 'twould be to be hurried back to Hamp-
shire!   95

HARRIET

    Ah! Name it not!

YOUNG BELLAIR

    As for us, I find we shall agree well enough. Would we could do
something to deceive the grave people!

HARRIET

    Could we delay their quick proceeding, 'twere well. A reprieve is
a good step towards the getting of a pardon.   100

YOUNG BELLAIR

    If we give over the game, we are undone. What think you of
playing it on booty?

HARRIET

    What do you mean?

YOUNG BELLAIR

    Pretend to be in love with one another. 'Twill make some dilat-
ory excuses we may feign pass the better.   105

HARRIET

    Let us do't, if it be but for the dear pleasure of dissembling.

YOUNG BELLAIR

    Can you play your part?

HARRIET

    I know not what it is to love, but I have made pretty remarks by
being now and then where lovers meet. Where did you leave
their gravities?   110

93 *hangings* wall-tapestries
108 *remarks* observations

---

102 *playing . . . on booty* joining with confederates to 'spoil' or victimize another
    player; to play into the hands of confederates in order to share the 'plunder'
    with them.

YOUNG BELLAIR

    I' the next room. Your mother was censuring our modern gallant.

Enter OLD BELLAIR *and* LADY WOODVILL

HARRIET

    Peace! Here they come. I will lean against this wall and look bashfully down upon my fan, while you, like an amorous spark, modishly entertain me.   115

LADY WOODVILL [*to* OLD BELLAIR]

    Never go about to excuse 'em. Come, come, it was not so when I was a young woman.

OLD BELLAIR

    Adod, they're something disrespectful—

LADY WOODVILL

    Quality was then considered, and not rallied by every fleering fellow.   120

OLD BELLAIR

    Youth will have its jest, adod it will.

LADY WOODVILL

    'Tis good breeding now to be civil to none but players and Exchange women. They are treated by 'em as much above their condition as others are below theirs.

OLD BELLAIR

    Out a pize on 'em! Talk no more: the rogues ha' got an ill habit of   125 preferring beauty, no matter where they find it.

LADY WOODVILL

    See, your son and my daughter. They have improved their acquaintance since they were within!

OLD BELLAIR

    Adod, methinks they have! Let's keep back and observe.

YOUNG BELLAIR [*to* HARRIET]

    Now for a look and gestures that may persuade 'em I am saying   130 all the passionate things imaginable.

HARRIET

    Your head a little more on one side. Ease yourself on your left leg and play with your right hand.

YOUNG BELLAIR

    Thus, is it not?

HARRIET

    Now set your right leg firm on the ground, adjust your belt, then   135 look about you.

119 *fleering* mocking, jeering
123 *Exchange women* women serving in the shops of the New Exchange

YOUNG BELLAIR

A little exercising will make me perfect.

HARRIET

Smile, and turn to me again very sparkish.

YOUNG BELLAIR

Will you take your turn and be instructed?

HARRIET

With all my heart. 140

YOUNG BELLAIR

At one motion play your fan, roll your eyes, and then settle a kind look upon me.

HARRIET

So.

YOUNG BELLAIR

Now spread your fan, look down upon it, and tell the sticks with a finger. 145

HARRIET

Very modish.

YOUNG BELLAIR

Clap your hand up to your bosom, hold down your gown. Shrug a little, draw up your breasts and let 'em fall again, gently, with a sigh or two, *etc.*

HARRIET

By the good instructions you give, I suspect you for one of those 150 malicious observers who watch people's eyes and from innocent looks make scandalous conclusions.

YOUNG BELLAIR

I know some, indeed, who out of mere love to mischief are as vigilant as jealousy itself, and will give you an account of every glance that passes at a play and i' the Circle. 155

HARRIET

'Twill not be amiss now to seem a little pleasant.

YOUNG BELLAIR

Clap your fan then in both your hands, snatch it to your mouth, smile, and with a lively motion fling your body a little forwards. So,—now spread it, fall back on the sudden, cover your face with it, and break out into a loud laughter.—Take up! Look 160 grave, and fall a-fanning of yourself. Admirably well acted!

HARRIET

I think I am pretty apt at these matters.

49 *etc.* Carnochan regards this as a stage direction, and comments, 'the actors were, evidently, to improvise'.

55 *the Circle* probably the 'Tour' or Ring in Hyde Park, used by the fashionable for riding and walking. Carnochan points out that the reference may possibly be to the assembly at Court (cf. IV.i, 120).

OLD BELLAIR [*to* LADY WOODVILL]
Adod, I like this well.

LADY WOODVILL
This promises something.

OLD BELLAIR [*coming forward*]
Come, there is love i' the case, adod there is, or will be.—What   165
say you, young lady?

HARRIET
All in good time, sir. You expect we should fall to and love as
gamecocks fight, as soon as we are set together. Adod, you're
unreasonable!

OLD BELLAIR
Adod, sirrah, I like thy wit well.   170

Enter a SERVANT

SERVANT
The coach is at the door, madam.

OLD BELLAIR
Go, get you and take the air together.

LADY WOODVILL
Will not you go with us?

OLD BELLAIR
Out a pize! Adod, I ha' business and cannot. We shall meet at
night at my sister Townley's.   175

YOUNG BELLAIR (*aside*)
He's going to Emilia. I overheard him talk of a collation.
Exeunt

Act III, Scene ii
[LADY TOWNLEY'S *house*]

Enter LADY TOWNLEY, EMILIA, *and* MEDLEY

LADY TOWNLEY
I pity the young lovers we last talked of, though to say truth,
their conduct has been so indiscreet they deserve to be unfortu-
nate.

MEDLEY
You have an exact account, from the great lady i' the box down to   5
the little orange-wench.

---

170 *sirrah* applied to a woman seriously or in jest up to 1711, but almost certainly
used here to indicate Old Bellair's old-fashioned vulgarity.

EMILIA

You're a living libel, a breathing lampoon. I wonder you are not torn in pieces.

MEDLEY

What think you of setting up an office of intelligence for these matters? The project may get money.

LADY TOWNLEY

You would have great dealings with country ladies.   10

MEDLEY

More than Muddiman has with their husbands.

Enter BELLINDA

LADY TOWNLEY

Bellinda, what has been become of you? We have not seen you here of late with your friend Mrs Loveit.

BELLINDA

Dear creature, I left her but now so sadly afflicted.

LADY TOWNLEY

With her old distemper, jealousy?   15

MEDLEY

Dorimant has played her some new prank.

BELLINDA

Well, that Dorimant is certainly the worst man breathing.

EMILIA

I once thought so.

BELLINDA

And do you not think so still?

EMILIA

No, indeed.   20

BELLINDA

Oh, Jesu!

EMILIA

The town does him a great deal of injury, and I will never believe what it says of a man I do not know again, for his sake.

6 *libel . . . lampoon* libel in the sense of a broadsheet or manuscript poem attacking a person's character, thus making it almost synonymous with lampoon, and supporting the pun on Medley being torn to pieces. Libels, which were often pinned to their victim's door, circulated in manuscript—Sir Roger L'Estrange complained in 1677 that 'it is notorious that not one in forty libels ever comes to the press, though by the help of manuscripts they are well-nigh as public' (quoted, *Poems of Affairs of State*, vol. I (1660–78), ed. G. de F. Lord (New Haven and London, 1963), p. xxxvii). See also I, 242–3 and note.

11 *Muddiman* Henry Muddiman (1629–92), first editor of the *London Gazette*, but referred to here for his newsletters, which had great popularity among country gentlemen.

BELLINDA

You make me wonder.

LADY TOWNLEY

He's a very well-bred man.   25

BELLINDA

But strangely ill-natured.

EMILIA

Then he's a very witty man.

BELLINDA

But a man of no principles.

MEDLEY

Your man of principles is a very fine thing, indeed!

BELLINDA

To be preferred to men of parts by women who have regard to   30
their reputation and quiet. Well, were I minded to play the fool,
he should be the last man I'd think of.

MEDLEY

He has been the first in many ladies' favours, though you are so
severe, madam.

LADY TOWNLEY

What he may be for a lover, I know not, but he's a very pleasant   35
acquaintance, I am sure.

BELLINDA

Had you seen him use Mrs Loveit as I have done, you would
never endure him more.

EMILIA

What, he has quarrelled with her again?

BELLINDA

Upon the slightest occasion. He's jealous of Sir Fopling.   40

LADY TOWNLEY

She never saw him in her life but yesterday, and that was here.

EMILIA

On my conscience, he's the only man in town that's her aversion.
How horribly out of humour she was all the while he talked to
her!

BELLINDA

And somebody has wickedly told him—   45

EMILIA

Here he comes.

Enter DORIMANT

MEDLEY

Dorimant, you are luckily come to justify yourself. Here's a
lady—

BELLINDA

—Has a word or two to say to you from a disconsolate person.

DORIMANT

You tender your reputation too much, I know, madam, to   50
whisper with me before this good company.

BELLINDA

To serve Mrs Loveit, I'll make a bold venture.

DORIMANT

Here's Medley, the very spirit of scandal.

BELLINDA

No matter!

EMILIA

'Tis something you are unwilling to hear, Mr Dorimant.   55

LADY TOWNLEY

Tell him, Bellinda, whether he will or no.

BELLINDA (*aloud*)

Mrs Loveit—

DORIMANT

Softly, these are laughers. You do not know 'em.

BELLINDA (*to* DORIMANT, *apart*)

In a word, you've made me hate you, which I thought you never
could have done.   60

DORIMANT

In obeying your commands.

BELLINDA

'Twas a cruel part you played. How could you act it?

DORIMANT

Nothing is cruel to a man who could kill himself to please you.
Remember, five o'clock tomorrow morning.

BELLINDA

I tremble when you name it.   65

DORIMANT

Be sure you come.

BELLINDA

I shan't.

DORIMANT

Swear you will.

BELLINDA

I dare not.

DORIMANT

Swear, I say!   70

BELLINDA

By my life, by all the happiness I hope for—

DORIMANT

You will.

BELLINDA
  I will.

DORIMANT
  Kind.

BELLINDA
  I am glad I've sworn. I vow I think I should ha' failed you else.   75

DORIMANT
  Surprisingly kind! In what temper did you leave Loveit?

BELLINDA
  Her raving was prettily over, and she began to be in a brave way
  of defying you and all your works. Where have you been since
  you went from thence?

DORIMANT
  I looked in at the play.   80

BELLINDA
  I have promised and must return to her again.

DORIMANT
  Persuade her to walk in the Mall this evening.

BELLINDA
  She hates the place and will not come.

DORIMANT
  Do all you can to prevail with her.

BELLINDA
  For what purpose?   85

DORIMANT
  Sir Fopling will be here anon. I'll prepare him to set upon her
  there before me.

BELLINDA
  You persecute her too much. But I'll do all you'll ha' me.

DORIMANT (*aloud*)
  Tell her plainly, 'tis grown so dull a business I can drudge on no
  longer.   90

EMILIA
  There are afflictions in love, Mr Dorimant.

DORIMANT
  You women make 'em, who are commonly as unreasonable in
  that as you are at play: without the advantage be on your side, a
  man can never quietly give over when he's weary.

MEDLEY
  If you would play without being obliged to complaisance,   95
  Dorimant, you should play in public places.

---

77 *prettily* cleverly, aptly

95 *complaisance* see note to I, 373.

DORIMANT

Ordinaries were a very good thing for that, but gentlemen do not of late frequent 'em. The deep play is now in private houses.

BELLINDA *offering to steal away*

LADY TOWNLEY

Bellinda, are you leaving us so soon?

BELLINDA

I am to go to the Park with Mrs Loveit, madam. [*Exit* BELLINDA]   100

LADY TOWNLEY

This confidence will go nigh to spoil this young creature.

MEDLEY

'Twill do her good, madam. Young men who are brought up under practising lawyers prove the abler counsel when they come to be called to the bar themselves.

DORIMANT

The town has been very favourable to you this afternoon, my   105
Lady Townley. You use to have an *embarras* of chairs and
coaches at your door, an uproar of footmen in your hall, and a
noise of fools above here.

LADY TOWNLEY

Indeed, my house is the general rendezvous and, next to the
playhouse, is the common refuge of all the young idle people.   110

EMILIA

Company is a very good thing, madam, but I wonder you do not
love it a little more chosen.

LADY TOWNLEY

'Tis good to have an universal taste. We should love wit, but for
variety be able to divert ourselves with the extravagancies of
those who want it.   115

MEDLEY

Fools will make you laugh.

EMILIA

For once or twice—but the repetition of their folly after a visit or
two grows tedious and insufferable.

LADY TOWNLEY

You are a little too delicate, Emilia.

---

97 *Ordinaries* eating houses, taverns
101 *confidence* excess of assurance, impudence (or, possibly, intimate relationship)

---

106 *embarras . . . coaches* cf. *embarras de voitures* (Fr.), a congestion of carriages.
Although 'embarras' (i.e. embarrassment) occurs as an uncommon English
word from 1664 into the eighteenth century, Q1's spelling 'ambara's' suggests
that Etherege intended the French word. It is used again by Sir Fopling (l.
165).

Enter a PAGE

PAGE
  Sir Fopling Flutter, madam, desires to know if you are to be   120
  seen.

LADY TOWNLEY
  Here's the freshest fool in town, and one who has not cloyed you
  yet.—Page!

PAGE
  Madam?

LADY TOWNLEY
  Desire him to walk up.   [*Exit* PAGE]   125

DORIMANT
  Do not you fall on him, Medley, and snub him. Soothe him up in
  his extravagance. He will show the better.

MEDLEY
  You know I have a natural indulgence for fools and need not this
  caution, sir.

Enter SIR FOPLING, *with his* PAGE *after him*

SIR FOPLING
  Page, wait without.   [*Exit* PAGE]   130
  ([*To*] LADY TOWNLEY) Madam, I kiss your hands. I see yesterday
  was nothing of chance; the *belles assemblées* form themselves here
  every day. (*To* EMILIA) Lady, your servant.—Dorimant, let me
  embrace thee. Without lying, I have not met with any of my
  acquaintance who retain so much of Paris as thou dost—the very   135
  air thou hadst when the marquise mistook thee i' the Tuileries
  and cried, '*Hé, chevalier!*' and then begged thy pardon.

DORIMANT
  I would fain wear in fashion as long as I can, sir. 'Tis a thing to be
  valued in men as well as baubles.

SIR FOPLING
  Thou art a man of wit and understands the town. Prithee, let   140
  thee and I be intimate. There is no living without making some
  good man the *confident* of our pleasures.

132 *belles assemblées* fashionable gatherings
140 *understands* Q1 (understand'st W, V)

126 *Soothe . . . up* encourage or humour a person by expressing assent or approval
    (1573–1705). *OED* cites this as an example.
136 *the Tuileries* the gardens of the Palais de Tuileries, laid out by Le Nôtre for
    Louis XIV, and so called because the palace occupied the site of an old
    brick-yard.

DORIMANT

'Tis true—but there is no man so improper for such a business as
I am.

SIR FOPLING

Prithee, why hast thou so modest an opinion of thyself?   145

DORIMANT

Why, first, I could never keep a secret in my life; and then, there
is no charm so infallibly makes me fall in love with a woman as
my knowing a friend loves her. I deal honestly with you.

SIR FOPLING

Thy humour's very gallant, or let me perish. I knew a French
count so like thee.   150

LADY TOWNLEY

Wit, I perceive, has more power over you than beauty, Sir
Fopling, else you would not have let this lady stand so long
neglected.

SIR FOPLING (*to* EMILIA)

A thousand pardons, madam—some civilities due of course
upon the meeting a long absent friend. The *éclat* of so much   155
beauty, I confess, ought to have charmed me sooner.

EMILIA

The *brillant* of so much good language, sir, has much more
power than the little beauty I can boast.

SIR FOPLING

I never saw anything prettier than this high work on your *point
d'Espagne*.   160

EMILIA

'Tis not so rich as *point de Venise*.

SIR FOPLING

Not altogether, but looks cooler, and is more proper for the
season.—Dorimant, is not that Medley?

DORIMANT

The same, sir.

---

154 *madam ... civilities* Q1 (madam. Some civility's Q2–3, CA)
155 *éclat* brilliance
157 *brillant* glitter
159 *high work* raised needlework
159–60 *point d'Espagne* Spanish lace
161 *point de Venise* Venetian lace

---

154 *madam ... of course* 'of course' means customary, natural, and Sir Fopling's
ellipsis can be paraphrased, 'My rudeness to you was occasioned by the need to
pay the customary civilities ...' Carnochan's emendation (see textual note)
gives the sense, 'some civility is naturally due ...', and is a possible reading.

SIR FOPLING [*to* MEDLEY]

Forgive me, sir; in this *embarras* of civilities I could not come to   165
have you in my arms sooner. You understand an equipage the
best of any man in town, I hear.

MEDLEY

By my own you would not guess it.

SIR FOPLING

There are critics who do not write, sir.

MEDLEY

Our peevish poets will scarce allow it.   170

SIR FOPLING

Damn 'em, they'll allow no man wit who does not play the fool
like themselves and show it! Have you taken notice of the gallesh
I brought over?

MEDLEY

Oh, yes! 'T has quite another air than the English makes.

SIR FOPLING

'Tis as easily known from an English tumbril as an Inns of Court   175
man is from one of us.

DORIMANT

Truly there is a *bel air* in galleshes as well as men.

MEDLEY

But there are few so delicate to observe it.

SIR FOPLING

The world is generally very *grossier* here, indeed.

---

165 *embarras* V, CA (Ambara's Q1ᵘ; Ambaras Q1ᶜ; the change may be meant to
suggest that Sir Fopling mispronounces the French) embarrassment

172 *gallesh* Q1 (*calèche* V)

175 *tumbril* two-wheeled cart which tips to empty its load, especially a dung-cart

175 *Inns of Court man* lawyer

177 *bel air* elegant style

177 *galleshes* Q1 (*calèshes* V)

179 *grossier* vulgar, coarse

---

166 *equipage* presumably in the sense of retinue, train of attendants (*OED*,
1590–1736), rather than apparel, costume. (Sir Fopling's comment at ll. 172–3
suggests that he could be thinking of 'equipage' as meaning his carriage and
attendants, but that appears to be an eighteenth-century usage).

172, 177 *gallesh* var. spelling of 'calash' from Fr. *calèche*: a light carriage with low
wheels and a removable folding hood or top. Newly introduced from France.
OED records the first occurrence in 1666, and Dryden's *Marriage-à-la-Mode*
(1673) has, 'I have been at your Lodgings in my new *Galeche*' (*Dramatic Works*,
ed. M. Summers (1931–32), vol. 3, 212).

178 *delicate* Dorimant plays on two meanings—1) fastidious, discerning, 2) dainty,
effeminate (obs.)

LADY TOWNLEY [*to* EMILIA]
  He's very fine.   180
EMILIA
  Extreme proper!
SIR FOPLING
  A slight suit I made to appear in at my first arrival—not worthy
  your consideration, ladies.
DORIMANT
  The pantaloon is very well mounted.
SIR FOPLING
  The tassels are new and pretty.   185
MEDLEY
  I never saw a coat better cut.
SIR FOPLING
  It makes me show long-waisted, and, I think, slender.
DORIMANT
  That's the shape our ladies dote on.
MEDLEY
  Your breech, though, is a handful too high, in my eye, Sir
  Fopling.   190
SIR FOPLING
  Peace, Medley, I have wished it lower a thousand times, but a
  pox on 't, 'twill not be!
LADY TOWNLEY
  His gloves are well fringed, large, and graceful.
SIR FOPLING
  I was always eminent for being *bien ganté*.
EMILIA
  He wears nothing but what are originals of the most famous   195
  hands in Paris.
SIR FOPLING
  You are in the right, madam.
LADY TOWNLEY
  The suit?

194 *bien ganté* well-gloved

---

184 *pantaloon* usually in plural, 'pantaloons': a kind of breeches in fashion after the
   Restoration, hanging wide down to the knees. Evelyn is cited by *OED* as saying
   in 1661, '... Pantaloons, which are a kind of Hermaphrodite and of neither
   sex'. Since Dorimant uses the singular, he may be playing on Pantaloon, the
   foolish old man in Italian harlequinade.
184 *mounted* Dorimant appears to be punning: 1) the breeches are well-mounted,
   that is, raised up away from the legs, 2) metaphorically, the ridiculous pantaloons are ridden (mounted) by an appropriate fool.

SIR FOPLING
  Barroy.
EMILIA
  The garniture?   200
SIR FOPLING
  Le Gras.
MEDLEY
  The shoes?
SIR FOPLING
  Piccar.
DORIMANT
  The periwig?
SIR FOPLING
  Chedreux.   205
LADY TOWNLEY, EMILIA
  The gloves?
SIR FOPLING
  Orangerie—you know the smell, ladies. —Dorimant, I could
  find in my heart for an amusement to have a gallantry with some
  of our English ladies.
DORIMANT
  'Tis a thing no less necessary to confirm the reputation of your 210
  wit than a duel will be to satisfy the town of your courage.
SIR FOPLING
  Here was a woman yesterday—
DORIMANT
  Mrs Loveit.
SIR FOPLING
  You have named her!
DORIMANT
  You cannot pitch on a better for your purpose.   215
SIR FOPLING
  Prithee, what is she?

199–205 *Barroy ... Chedreux* of this list of fashionable Parisian merchants I can
     identify only Chedreux, who gave his name to a kind of wig.
200 *garniture* ornament, trimming of ribbons and jewellery, added to clothing.
     Strongly connected to its French origins at this date. First example in *OED* is
     from 1667. J. Lacey's *Sir Hercules Buffoon* (1684) has, 'My French garniture, a
     pox on 'em, is not yet arrived from Paris' (II.ii).
207 *Orangerie* scent or perfume extracted from the orange-flower. *OED* records
     this instance as its first occurrence. Essence of orange was a popular scent, and
     in Dryden's *The Kind Keeper* (1680) Mrs Tricksy tells Limberham, 'I have
     been looking over the last present of *Orange* Gloves you made me; and
     methinks I do not like the scent' (III.i). A quart of orange-flower water is
     included in the effects of a fop in *Tatler*, No. 113. See also note to V.i, 34.

DORIMANT

A person of quality, and one who has a rest of reputation enough to make the conquest considerable. Besides I hear she likes you too.

SIR FOPLING

Methoughts she seemed, though, very reserved and uneasy all 220
the time I entertained her.

DORIMANT

Grimace and affectation! You will see her i' the Mall tonight.

SIR FOPLING

Prithee, let thee and I take the air together.

DORIMANT

I am engaged to Medley, but I'll meet you at St James's and give you some information upon the which you may regulate your 225
proceedings.

SIR FOPLING

All the world will be in the Park tonight. —Ladies, 'twere pity to keep so much beauty longer within doors and rob the Ring of all those charms that should adorn it. —Hey, page!

Enter PAGE

See that all my people be ready.   [PAGE] *goes out again* 230
Dorimant, *à revoir*.   [*Exit* SIR FOPLING]

MEDLEY

A fine-mettled coxcomb.

DORIMANT

Brisk and insipid—

MEDLEY

Pert and dull.

EMILIA

However you despise him, gentlemen, I'll lay my life he passes 235
for a wit with many.

---

217 *rest* remainder
229–30 s.d. *Enter . . . again* CA (Q1 and all other texts give as a single sentence after
l. 229)
231 *à revoir* ed. (a Revoir Q1; *au revoir* V, CA)

---

228 *the Ring* see note to III.i, 155
231 *à revoir* in following Q1 here the text adopts Brian Gibbons's shrewd observation that since Dorimant mocks Sir Fopling's usage (l. 246), the knight is
probably pretending that his is the fashionable pronunciation of the phrase in
Paris. Or it may be an example of his 'pretty lisp' (I, 327).

DORIMANT

That may very well be. Nature has her cheats, stums a brain, and puts sophisticate dullness often on the tasteless multitude for true wit and good humour. —Medley, come.

MEDLEY

I must go a little way. I will meet you i' the Mall.   240

DORIMANT

I'll walk through the garden thither. (*To the women*) We shall meet anon and bow.

LADY TOWNLEY

Not tonight. We are engaged about a business, the knowledge of which may make you laugh hereafter.

MEDLEY

Your servant, ladies.   245

DORIMANT

À revoir, as Sir Fopling says.

                    [*Exeunt* MEDLEY *and* DORIMANT]

LADY TOWNLEY

The old man will be here immediately.

EMILIA

Let's expect him i' the garden.

LADY TOWNLEY

Go, you are a rogue!

EMILIA

I can't abide you!   *Exeunt*   250

Act III, Scene iii
The Mall

Enter HARRIET *and* YOUNG BELLAIR, *she pulling him*

HARRIET

Come along!

246 *À revoir* ed. (a Revoir Q1; *au revoir* V, CA)
248 *expect* wait for

---

237 *stum* to renew (wine) by mixing with stum or must and raising a new fermentation (from the Dutch). *OED* gives first occurrence as 1656, and the first figurative use in 1661. Oldham's *Letter from the Country* (1678) has, 'As the poor Drunkard, when Wine stums his brains, /Anointed with that Liquor, thinks he reigns'.

238 *sophisticate* probably in the obsolescent sense, 'adulterated, impure, mixed with some foreign substance'. The last example given by the *OED* is from Maynwaring's *Ancient and Modern Practice of Physick* (1671), 66, 'Yet this cheap sophisticate Medicine . . . will cost you six times as much'. This sense would continue Dorimant's metaphor of adulterated wine passed off upon the 'tasteless multitude'.

YOUNG BELLAIR

And leave your mother?

HARRIET

Busy will be sent with a hue and cry after us; but that's no matter.

YOUNG BELLAIR

'Twill look strangely in me.   5

HARRIET

She'll believe it a freak of mine and never blame your manners.

YOUNG BELLAIR [*pointing*]

What reverend acquaintance is that she has met?

HARRIET

A fellow beauty of the last king's time, though by the ruins you would hardly guess it.   *Exeunt*

> *Enter* DORIMANT *and crosses the stage*
> *Enter* YOUNG BELLAIR *and* HARRIET

YOUNG BELLAIR

By this time your mother is in a fine taking.   10

HARRIET

If your friend Mr Dorimant were but here now, that she might find me talking with him!

YOUNG BELLAIR

She does not know him but dreads him, I hear, of all mankind.

HARRIET

She concludes if he does but speak to a woman, she's undone—is on her knees every day to pray heaven defend me from him.   15

YOUNG BELLAIR

You do not apprehend him so much as she does?

HARRIET

I never saw anything in him that was frightful.

YOUNG BELLAIR

On the contrary, have you not observed something extreme delightful in his wit and person?

HARRIET

He's agreeable and pleasant, I must own, but he does so much   20
affect being so, he displeases me.

YOUNG BELLAIR

Lord, madam, all he does and says is so easy and so natural.

HARRIET

Some men's verses seem so to the unskilful; but labour i' the one and affectation in the other to the judicious plainly appear.

6 *freak* whim, capricious humour
10 *taking* excited or impassioned state

YOUNG BELLAIR
   I never heard him accused of affectation before.   25

          Enter DORIMANT *and stares upon her*

HARRIET
   It passes on the easy town, who are favourably pleased in him to
   call it humour.   [*Exeunt* YOUNG BELLAIR *and* HARRIET]
DORIMANT
   'Tis she! It must be she—that lovely hair, that easy shape, those
   wanton eyes, and all those melting charms about her mouth
   which Medley spoke of. I'll follow the lottery and put in for a   30
   prize with my friend Bellair.
          [*Exit* DORIMANT, *repeating*]—
   'In love the victors from the vanquished fly;
   They fly that wound, and they pursue that die'.

          Enter YOUNG BELLAIR *and* HARRIET, *and after them* DORIMANT,
          standing at a distance

YOUNG BELLAIR
   Most people prefer Hyde Park to this place.
HARRIET
   It has the better reputation, I confess; but I abominate the dull   35
   diversions there—the formal bows, the affected smiles, the silly
   by-words and amorous tweers in passing. Here one meets with a
   little conversation now and then.
YOUNG BELLAIR
   These conversations have been fatal to some of your sex,
   madam.   40
HARRIET
   It may be so. Because some who want temper have been undone

26 *passes on* goes uncensured by
41 *temper* character, self-control

26, 28 *easy* see note to I, 119, and Introduction, p. xxxiii.
28–30 *'Tis ... of* see I, 117–25 and notes.
30 *the lottery* common way of raising money for the government or for individuals.
32–3 *In ... die* final couplet of Waller's 'To a Friend, of the Different Successes of
   their Loves' (*Poems*, ed. G. Thorn Drury (1901), vol. 1, 103).
34 *Hyde Park* Etherege's form *High Park*, here and at V.ii, 138, is unusual and
   probably went out of use by the early eighteenth century. Brett-Smith knew of
   no occurrences outside Etherege, but Conaghan cites Lady Margaret Cavend-
   ish's *A Piece of a Play*, 'Madam, are you for a Play? or Court? or *High-Park* to
   day?' (*Plays* (1668), p. 14).
37 *tweer* var. spelling of 'twire', a glance, leer (obs. slang). *OED* gives this as first
   occurrence (the last is from 1719), but the verb occurs from 1600, and
   remained in dialect until the nineteenth century.

by gaming, must others who have it wholly deny themselves the pleasure of play?

DORIMANT (*coming up gently and bowing to her*)

Trust me, it were unreasonable, madam.

HARRIET

Lord! Who's this?   *She starts and looks grave*   45

YOUNG BELLAIR

Dorimant.

DORIMANT

Is this the woman your father would have you marry?

YOUNG BELLAIR

It is.

DORIMANT

Her name?

YOUNG BELLAIR

Harriet.   50

DORIMANT [*aside*]

I am not mistaken. —She's handsome.

YOUNG BELLAIR

Talk to her; her wit is better than her face. We were wishing for you but now.

DORIMANT (*to* HARRIET)

Overcast with seriousness o' the sudden! A thousand smiles were shining in that face but now—I never saw so quick a change of   55
weather.

HARRIET (*aside*)

I feel as great a change within, but he shall never know it.

DORIMANT

You were talking of play, madam. Pray, what may be your stint?

HARRIET

A little harmless discourse in public walks, or at most an appointment in a box, barefaced, at the playhouse. You are for   60
masks and private meetings, where women engage for all they are worth, I hear.

DORIMANT

I have been used to deep play, but I can make one at small game when I like my gamester well.

HARRIET

And be so unconcerned you'll ha' no pleasure in 't.   65

DORIMANT

Where there is a considerable sum to be won, the hope of drawing people in makes every trifle considerable.

---

58 *stint* upper limit

HARRIET

The sordidness of men's natures, I know, makes 'em willing to flatter and comply with the rich, though they are sure never to be the better for 'em.   70

DORIMANT

'Tis in their power to do us good, and we despair not but at some time or other they may be willing.

HARRIET

To men who have fared in this town like you, 'twould be a great mortification to live on hope. Could you keep a Lent for a mistress?   75

DORIMANT

In expectation of a happy Easter, and though time be very precious, think forty days well lost to gain your favour.

HARRIET

Mr Bellair! Let us walk. 'Tis time to leave him. Men grow dull when they begin to be particular.

DORIMANT

You're mistaken. Flattery will not ensue, though I know you're   80
greedy of the praises of the whole Mall.

HARRIET

You do me wrong.

DORIMANT

I do not. As I followed you, I observed how you were pleased when the fops cried 'She's handsome, very handsome, by God she is!' and whispered aloud your name—the thousand several   85
forms you put your face into; then, to make yourself more agreeable, how wantonly you played with your head, flung back your locks, and looked smilingly over your shoulder at 'em.

HARRIET

I do not go begging the men's, as you do the ladies' good liking, with a sly softness in your looks and a gentle slowness in your   90
bows as you pass by 'em. As thus, sir—(*Acts him*) Is not this like you?

Enter LADY WOODVILL *and* BUSY

YOUNG BELLAIR

Your mother, madam!   *Pulls* HARRIET. *She composes herself*

LADY WOODVILL

Ah, my dear child Harriet!

85–6 *name*— ... *into;* CA (name, ... into; Q1; name; ... into; B)

---

68 *sordidness* low, mean, or mercenary character or motives.

BUSY [*aside*]

    Now is she so pleased with finding her again, she cannot chide   95
her.

LADY WOODVILL

    Come away!

DORIMANT

    'Tis now but high Mall, madam—the most entertaining time of
all the evening.

HARRIET

    I would fain see that Dorimant, mother, you so cry out of for a   100
monster. He's in the Mall, I hear.

LADY WOODVILL

    Come away, then! The plague is here, and you should dread the
infection.

YOUNG BELLAIR

    You may be misinformed of the gentleman.

LADY WOODVILL

    Oh, no! I hope you do not know him. He is the prince of all the   105
devils in the town—delights in nothing but in rapes and riots.

DORIMANT

    If you did but hear him speak, madam—

LADY WOODVILL

    Oh, he has a tongue, they say, would tempt the angels to a second
fall.

Enter SIR FOPLING *with his equipage, six footmen and a page*

SIR FOPLING

    Hey, Champagne, Norman, La Rose, La Fleur, La Tour, La   110
Verdure!—Dorimant!—

LADY WOODVILL

    Here, here he is among this rout! He names him!— Come away,
Harriet, come away!

Exeunt LADY WOODVILL, HARRIET, BUSY, *and* YOUNG BELLAIR

DORIMANT [*aside*]

    This fool's coming has spoiled all. She's gone, but she has left a
pleasing image of herself behind that wanders in my soul.— It   115
must not settle there.

100 *of* Q1 (V omits)

---

98 *high Mall* the busiest and most fashionable hour for visiting the Mall.
109 s.d. *equipage* here 'retinue', but see note to III.ii, 166.
110 *Champagne ... Verdure* see note to III.iii, 252–3, which accounts for some of
    these names. On 'champagne' see note to IV.i, 371.

SIR FOPLING
  What reverie is this? Speak, man.
DORIMANT
       'Snatched from myself, how far behind
         Already I behold the shore!'

                    Enter MEDLEY

MEDLEY
  Dorimant, a discovery! I met with Bellair—   120
DORIMANT
  You can tell me no news, sir. I know all.
MEDLEY
  How do you like the daughter?
DORIMANT
  You never came so near truth in your life as you did in her
  description.
MEDLEY
  What think you of the mother?   125
DORIMANT
  Whatever I think of her, she thinks very well of me, I find.
MEDLEY
  Did she know you?
DORIMANT
  She did not. Whether she does now or no, I know not. Here was a
  pleasant scene towards, when in came Sir Fopling, mustering up
  his equipage, and at the latter end named me and frighted her   130
  away.
MEDLEY
  Loveit and Bellinda are not far off. I saw 'em alight at St James's.
DORIMANT
  Sir Fopling, hark you, a word or two. (*Whispers*)—Look you do
  not want assurance.
SIR FOPLING
  I never do on these occasions.   135

---

129 *towards* imminent

---

117 *reverie* bears the modern meaning, but in Middle English it had meant 'revel-
   ling, rejoicing', and was readopted from French *rèverie* in the seventeenth
   century. *OED* records its first instance from 1657, but it retained a strong sense
   of its French origin into the eighteenth century.
118–19 *Snatched . . . shore* Waller, 'Of Loving at First Sight', ll. 3–4 (*Poems*, ed. G.
   Thorn Drury (1901), vol. 1, 100).
132 *St James's* Carnochan thinks the reference is to St James's Palace, opposite the
   Park.

DORIMANT

Walk on, we must not be seen together. Make your advantage of what I have told you. The next turn you will meet the lady.

SIR FOPLING

Hey! Follow me all.   *Exeunt* SIR FOPLING *and his equipage*

DORIMANT

Medley, you shall see good sport anon between Loveit and this Fopling.   140

MEDLEY

I thought there was something toward, by that whisper.

DORIMANT

You know a worthy principle of hers?

MEDLEY

Not to be so much as civil to a man who speaks to her in the presence of him she professes to love.

DORIMANT

I have encouraged Fopling to talk to her tonight.   145

MEDLEY

Now you are here, she will go nigh to beat him.

DORIMANT

In the humour she's in, her love will make her do some very extravagant thing, doubtless.

MEDLEY

What was Bellinda's business with you at my Lady Townley's?

DORIMANT

To get me to meet Loveit here in order to an *éclaircissement*. I   150
made some difficulty of it and have prepared this rencounter to make good my jealousy.

MEDLEY

Here they come.

          Enter MRS LOVEIT, BELLINDA, *and* PERT

DORIMANT

I'll meet her and provoke her with a deal of dumb civility in

---

137 *next turn* next circuit of the Mall
150 *éclaircissement* clearing up (of a mystery, misunderstanding)

---

151 *rencounter* chance meeting is the primary meaning, but the word could also mean a military skirmish, a duel, or a contest in wit or argument (*OED*). Verity emends to *rencontre* (unnecessarily since Q1's 'rancounter' is a variant spelling of 'rencounter').

passing by, then turn short and be behind her when Sir Fopling   155
sets upon her—[*Bows to* MRS LOVEIT]

> 'See how unregarded now
> That piece of beauty passes'.

Exeunt DORIMANT *and* MEDLEY

BELLINDA

How wonderful respectfully he bowed!

PERT

He's always over-mannerly when he has done a mischief.   160

BELLINDA

Methoughts, indeed, at the same time he had a strange, despising countenance.

PERT

The unlucky look he thinks becomes him.

BELLINDA

I was afraid you would have spoke to him, my dear.

MRS LOVEIT

I would have died first. He shall no more find me the loving fool   165
he has done.

BELLINDA

You love him still!

MRS LOVEIT

No.

PERT

I wish you did not.

MRS LOVEIT

I do not, and I will have you think so!— What made you hale me   170
to this odious place, Bellinda?

BELLINDA

I hate to be hulched up in a coach. Walking is much better.

MRS LOVEIT

Would we could meet Sir Fopling now!

BELLINDA

Lord, would you not avoid him?

MRS LOVEIT

I would make him all the advances that may be.   175

BELLINDA

That would confirm Dorimant's suspicion, my dear.

163 *unlucky* mischievous, malicious

157–8 *See ... passes* Suckling, 'Sonnet I', ll. 1–2, which actually begins 'Do'st ...'
(*Sir John Suckling, The Non-Dramatic Works*, ed. Thomas Clayton (Oxford
1971), p. 47).

172 *hulched up* doubled up (obs.). *OED* gives this as the only example of the verb
formed from 'hulch', hunch-backed (1611–1708).

MRS LOVEIT

He is not jealous, but I will make him so, and be revenged a way
he little thinks on.

BELLINDA (*aside*)

If she should make him jealous, that may make him fond of her
again. I must dissuade her from it.— Lord, my dear, this will   180
certainly make him hate you.

MRS LOVEIT

'Twill make him uneasy, though he does not care for me. I know
the effects of jealousy on men of his proud temper.

BELLINDA

'Tis a fantastic remedy: its operations are dangerous and uncertain.   185

MRS LOVEIT

'Tis the strongest cordial we can give to dying love. It often
brings it back when there's no sign of life remaining. But I design
not so much the reviving his, as my revenge.

Enter SIR FOPLING *and his equipage*

SIR FOPLING

Hey! Bid the coachman send home four of his horses and bring
the coach to Whitehall. I'll walk over the Park. [*To* MRS LOVEIT]   190
Madam, the honour of kissing your fair hands is a happiness I
missed this afternoon at my Lady Townley's.

MRS LOVEIT

You were very obliging, Sir Fopling, the last time I saw you
there.

SIR FOPLING

The preference was due to your wit and beauty. [*To* BELLINDA]   195
Madam, your servant. There never was so sweet an evening.

BELLINDA

'T has drawn all the rabble of the town hither.

SIR FOPLING

'Tis pity there's not an order made that none but the *beau monde*
should walk here.

---

186 *cordial* medicine or beverage to stimulate the heart

186–7 *'Tis . . . remaining* cf. Etherege's 'Song' (Tell me no more you love; in vain),
    ll. 13–16, 'Each smile and kiss which you bestow,/Are like those cordials which
    we give/To dying men, to make them live,/And languish out an hour in pain'
    (Thorpe, p. 24). First published 1669.
190 *Whitehall* royal palace, burned down in 1698. It was across St James's Park
    from the Mall.

MRS LOVEIT
'Twould add much to the beauty of the place. See what a sort of   200
nasty fellows are coming!

Enter four ill-fashioned fellows singing:
'''Tis not for kisses alone, etc.'*

MRS LOVEIT
Foh! Their periwigs are scented with tobacco so strong—

SIR FOPLING
—It overcomes our pulvilio. Methinks I smell the coffee-house
they come from.   205

FIRST MAN
Dorimant's convenient, Madam Loveit.

SECOND MAN
I like the oily buttock with her.

THIRD MAN [*pointing to* SIR FOPLING]
What spruce prig is that?

---

201 s.d. *four* (three V)
208 *spruce prig* fop, coxcomb (slang)

---

200 *sort* either 1) variety, kind, or 2) body (of people), company (obs.). The latter
meaning persisted into the nineteenth century (*OED* 17c), though Conaghan
cites E. Fenton (1730), who felt the usage old-fashioned. See following note.

201 s.d. *four* the number is given as 'three' in the Dramatis Personae, and Verity
emends here to match. Conaghan, noting that 'sort' (l. 200) could mean
'crowd', argues for the present reading—'The author may have considered the
theatrical effectiveness of having the "nasty Fellows" outnumber the people of
fashion on stage'. Since the text of Q1 descends from an authorial manuscript
(see Note on the Text), the cast list, which unlike the earlier part of Q1
distinguishes between Young and Old Bellair, must have been prepared after
the text. Cutting the 'ill-fashioned fellows' from four to three probably reflects
an economy made for production.

202, 211 *'Tis . . . etc., There's . . . etc.* Lines from the second stanza of an anonymous
song, 'Tell me no more you love'. For the words and source see Appendix B.

204 *pulvilio* scented powder (from It. 'polviglio'). A new word: *OED* gives its first
example from Wycherley's *The Country Wife* (1675).

206 *convenient* mistress (obs.). Earliest of *OED*'s three examples. Cf. P. Motteux,
Rabelais (1708; 1737 ed.), vol. 5, 217, 'Concubines, Convenients, Cracks'.

207 *oily buttock* 'buttock' was slang for a whore. James Dalton in *A Narrative . . .*
(1728) defines a 'Buttock' as 'One that dispenses her Favours without Advantage', i.e., free of charge. 'Oily' could mean greasy or smooth in manner,
'slippery'. Most obviously the bully refers to Bellinda, but Mrs Loveit apparently knows one of them by sight (ll. 229–30), and the reference is conceivably
to her.

FIRST MAN

A caravan, lately come from Paris.

SECOND MAN

Peace, they smoke!   *All of them coughing*   210
'There's something else to be done, etc.'
                                        Exeunt singing

Enter DORIMANT *and* MEDLEY

DORIMANT

They're engaged—

MEDLEY

She entertains him as if she liked him.

DORIMANT

Let us go forward, seem earnest in discourse, and show ourselves. Then you shall see how she'll use him.   215

BELLINDA

Yonder's Dorimant, my dear.

MRS LOVEIT

I see him. (*Aside*) He comes insulting, but I will disappoint him
in his expectation. (*To* SIR FOPLING)—I like this pretty, nice
humour of yours, Sir Fopling. [*To* BELLINDA] With what a
loathing eye he looked upon those fellows!   220

SIR FOPLING

I sat near one of 'em at a play today and was almost poisoned with
a pair of cordovan gloves he wears.

MRS LOVEIT

Oh, filthy cordovan! How I hate the smell!
                                        Laughs in a loud, affected way

SIR FOPLING

Did you observe, madam, how their cravats hung loose an inch
from their neck, and what a frightful air it gave 'em?   225

MRS LOVEIT

Oh! I took particular notice of one that is always spruced up with
a deal of dirty, sky-coloured ribbon.

---

10 *smoke* take note, 'twig'

09 *caravan* object of plunder (thieves' cant). *OED* gives first example, however,
from Shadwell, *Squire of Alsatia* (1688), and also cites B. E., *Dictionary of the
Canting Crew* (1690), '*Caravan*, a good round Sum of Money about a Man, and
him that is cheated of it'.

11 *There's ... etc.* see note to l. 202 above.

22 *cordovan* a Spanish leather, originally made from tanned and dressed goatskins,
but later from split horse-hides (cf. 'cordwain', *OED*). Q1 spells 'cordivant'.

BELLINDA
     That's one of the walking flageolets who haunt the Mall o' nights.
MRS LOVEIT
     Oh, I remember him! He has a hollow tooth, enough to spoil the
     sweetness of an evening.   230
SIR FOPLING
     I have seen the tallest walk the streets with a dainty pair of boxes,
     neatly buckled on.
MRS LOVEIT
     And a little footboy at his heels, pocket-high, with a flat cap, a
     dirty face—
SIR FOPLING
     —And a snotty nose.   235
MRS LOVEIT
     Oh, odious! There's many of my own sex, with that Holborn
     equipage, trig to Gray's Inn Walks, and now and then travel
     hither on a Sunday.
MEDLEY [to DORIMANT]
     She takes no notice of you.
DORIMANT
     Damn her! I am jealous of a counterplot.   240
MRS LOVEIT
     Your liveries are the finest, Sir Fopling. Oh, that page! that page
     is the prettily'st dressed. They are all Frenchmen?
SIR FOPLING
     There's one damned English blockhead among 'em. You may
     know him by his mien.

229 *He has* ed. (H' has Q1; He's V, B)   237 *trig* Q1 (trip V) dress smartly

---

228 *flageolet* a relation of the recorder with six fingerholes, invented in France. 'The
    flageolet was popular in England from about 1666 until it was set aside in favour
    of the recorder some fifteen years later' (*Grove's Dictionary*). Pepys played the
    flageolet.
229 *He has ... tooth* Brett-Smith defends his reading, which makes the hollow tooth
    a metaphor for the man, by citing Sparkish's calling Lucy in *The Country Wife*
    (1675), V.iv, an 'eternal Rotten-tooth'.
231 *boxes* Carnochan suggests, 'wooden overshoes (?)'. The *OED* is of no help, but
    the reference is to some unfashionable form of footwear.
233 *flat cap* round cap with a low, flat crown, worn in the sixteenth and seventeenth
    centuries by London citizens, especially apprentices.
236–7 *Holborn equipage* unfashionable retinue characteristic of the City. Holborn
    was a centre of commerce and business.
237 *Gray's Inn Walks* gardens of Gray's Inn, an Inn of Court in Holborn, notorious
    as a place for assignations.
244 *mien* Sir Fopling may be using the French word *mine* (Q1 spells 'Meine'): in
    Etherege's earlier plays the word is spelt both 'mine' and 'meen'.

MRS LOVEIT
Oh, that's he, that's he! What do you call him?   245
SIR FOPLING [*calling* FOOTMAN]
Hey!—I know not what to call him.
MRS LOVEIT
What's your name?
FOOTMAN
John Trott, madam.
SIR FOPLING
Oh, insufferable! Trott, Trott, Trott! There's nothing so bar-
barous as the names of our English servants. What countryman 250
are you, sirrah?
FOOTMAN
Hampshire, sir.
SIR FOPLING
Then Hampshire be your name. Hey, Hampshire!
MRS LOVEIT
Oh, that sound! That sound becomes the mouth of a man of
quality.   255
MEDLEY
Dorimant, you look a little bashful on the matter.
DORIMANT
She dissembles better than I thought she could have done.
MEDLEY
You have tempted her with too luscious a bait. She bites at the
coxcomb.
DORIMANT
She cannot fall from loving me to that?   260

250 *countryman* i.e., which country do you come from?
252-3 *Hampshire* Brett-Smith draws attention to Congreve's reference: 'The
Ancients us'd to call their Servants by the names of the Countries from whence
they came ... The *French* to this Day do the same, and call their Footmen
Champagne[,]*le Picard, le Gascon, le Bourgignon*, &c. and Sir *George Etheridge* in
his Sir *Fopling Flutter*, the *Hampshire*, &c. speaking to his Valet imitates this
Custom' ('Notes on the Third Book of *Ovid's Art of Love*', *Ovid's Art of Love in
Three Books ... By Several Eminent Hands* (1709), pp. 253-4).

MEDLEY

You begin to be jealous in earnest.

DORIMANT

Of one I do not love?

MEDLEY

You did love her.

DORIMANT

The fit has long been over.

MEDLEY

But I have known men fall into dangerous relapses when they   26.
have found a woman inclining to another.

DORIMANT (*to himself*)

He guesses the secret of my heart. I am concerned but dare not
show it, lest Bellinda should mistrust all I have done to gain her.

BELLINDA (*aside*)

I have watched his look and find no alteration there. Did he love
her, some signs of jealousy would have appeared.   27.

DORIMANT [*to* MRS LOVEIT]

I hope this happy evening, madam, has reconciled you to the
scandalous Mall. We shall have you now hankering here again.

MRS LOVEIT

Sir Fopling, will you walk?

SIR FOPLING

I am all obedience, madam.

MRS LOVEIT

Come along then, and let's agree to be malicious on all the   27.
ill-fashioned things we meet.

SIR FOPLING

We'll make a critique on the whole Mall, madam.

MRS LOVEIT

Bellinda, you shall engage—

BELLINDA

To the reserve of our friends, my dear.

MRS LOVEIT

No! No exceptions.   28.

SIR FOPLING

We'll sacrifice all to our diversion.

---

272 *hankering* 'hanging about'   278 *engage* participate
277 *critique* CA (Critick Q1; *critique* V) 279 *To . . . of* with the exception of

---

277 *critique* probably not the French word (see textual note). *OED*'s first example
is from Addison (1702–21). The normal English spelling was 'critick' (and so
pronounced); it altered to the French spelling during the eighteenth century,
and was given the French pronunciation in the nineteenth.

MRS LOVEIT
  All—all—
SIR FOPLING
  All!
BELLINDA
  All? Then let it be.

Exeunt SIR FOPLING, MRS LOVEIT, BELLINDA, *and* PERT, *laughing*

MEDLEY
  Would you had brought some more of your friends, Dorimant,   285
  to have been witnesses of Sir Fopling's disgrace and your
  triumph!
DORIMANT
  'Twere unreasonable to desire you not to laugh at me, but pray
  do not expose me to the town this day or two.
MEDLEY
  By that time you hope to have regained your credit?   290
DORIMANT
  I know she hates Fopling and only makes use of him in hope to
  work me on again. Had it not been for some powerful considerations which will be removed tomorrow morning, I had
  made her pluck off this mask and show the passion that lies
  panting under.   295

Enter a FOOTMAN

MEDLEY
  Here comes a man from Bellair, with news of your last adven-
  ture.
DORIMANT
  I am glad he sent him. I long to know the consequence of our
  parting.
FOOTMAN
  Sir, my master desires you to come to my Lady Townley's   300
  presently and bring Mr Medley with you. My Lady Woodvill
  and her daughter are there.
MEDLEY
  Then all's well, Dorimant.
FOOTMAN
  They have sent for the fiddles and mean to dance. He bid me tell
  you, sir, the old lady does not know you, and would have you   305
  own yourself to be Mr Courtage. They are all prepared to receive
  you by that name.

301 *presently* immediately

DORIMANT

That foppish admirer of quality, who flatters the very meat at honourable tables and never offers love to a woman below a lady-grandmother!   310

MEDLEY

You know the character you are to act, I see.

DORIMANT

This is Harriet's contrivance—wild, witty, lovesome, beautiful, and young.— Come along, Medley.

MEDLEY

This new woman would well supply the loss of Loveit.

DORIMANT

That business must not end so. Before tomorrow sun is set, I will   315 revenge and clear it.

> And you and Loveit, to her cost, shall find
> I fathom all the depths of womankind.   *Exeunt*

312–13 *wild ... young* Brett-Smith compares with Waller, 'Of the Danger his Majesty (Being Prince) Escaped in the Road at Saint Andrews', ll. 13–14: 'Of the Fourth Edward was his noble song,/Fierce, goodly, valiant, beautiful, and young' (ed. G. Thorn Drury (1901), vol. 1, 1).

Act IV, Scene i
[LADY TOWNLEY's *house*]

The scene opens with the fiddles playing a country dance

Enter DORIMANT [*and*] LADY WOODVILL, YOUNG BELLAIR *and*
MRS HARRIET, OLD BELLAIR *and* EMILIA, MR MEDLEY *and* LADY
TOWNLEY, *as having just ended the dance*

OLD BELLAIR
So, so, so! A smart bout, a very smart bout, adod!
LADY TOWNLEY
How do you like Emilia's dancing, brother?
OLD BELLAIR
Not at all, not at all!
LADY TOWNLEY
You speak not what you think, I am sure.
OLD BELLAIR
No matter for that—go, bid her dance no more. It don't become   5
her, it don't become her. Tell her I say so. (*Aside*) Adod, I love
her.
DORIMANT (*to* LADY WOODVILL)
All people mingle nowadays, madam. And in public places
women of quality have the least respect showed 'em.
LADY WOODVILL
I protest you say the truth, Mr Courtage.   10
DORIMANT
Forms and ceremonies, the only things that uphold quality and
greatness, are now shamefully laid aside and neglected.
LADY WOODVILL
Well, this is not the women's age, let 'em think what they will.
Lewdness is the business now; love was the business in my time.
DORIMANT
The women, indeed, are little beholding to the young men of this   15
age. They're generally only dull admirers of themselves and
make their court to nothing but their periwigs and their
cravats—and would be more concerned for the disordering of
'em, though on a good occasion, than a young maid would be for
the tumbling of her head or handkercher.   20

15 *beholding* Q1 (beholden Q3)
20 *handkercher* Q1 (handkerchief W, V) unusual variant of 'handkerchief' (not in
    OED), meaning here a kerchief for the neck or head

LADY WOODVILL
  I protest you hit 'em.

DORIMANT
  They are very assiduous to show themselves at court, well-
  dressed, to the women of quality; but their business is with the
  stale mistresses of the town, who are prepared to receive their
  lazy addresses by industrious old lovers who have cast 'em off   25
  and made 'em easy.

HARRIET [to MEDLEY]
  He fits my mother's humour so well, a little more and she'll
  dance a kissing dance with him anon.

MEDLEY
  Dutifully observed, madam.

DORIMANT
  They pretend to be great critics in beauty—by their talk you   30
  would think they liked no face—and yet can dote on an ill one if it
  belong to a laundress or a tailor's daughter. They cry a woman's
  past her prime at twenty, decayed at four-and-twenty, old and
  insufferable at thirty.

LADY WOODVILL
  Insufferable at thirty! That they are in the wrong, Mr Courtage,   35
  at five-and-thirty there are living proofs enough to convince 'em.

DORIMANT
  Ay, madam! There's Mrs Setlooks, Mrs Droplip, and my Lady
  Loud. Show me among all our opening buds a face that promises
  so much beauty as the remains of theirs.

LADY WOODVILL
  The depraved appetite of this vicious age tastes nothing but   40
  green fruit and loathes it when 'tis kindly ripened.

DORIMANT
  Else so many deserving women, madam, would not be so
  untimely neglected.

LADY WOODVILL
  I protest, Mr Courtage, a dozen such good men as you would be
  enough to atone for that wicked Dorimant and all the under-   45
  debauchees of the town. (HARRIET, EMILIA, YOUNG BELLAIR,
  MEDLEY [and] LADY TOWNLEY break out into a laughter)—What's
  the matter there?

---

41 *kindly* naturally, seasonably

---

28 *kissing dance* i.e., cushion-dance, a round dance formerly danced at weddings,
  in which the men and women alternately knelt on a cushion to be kissed.
  Referred to as 'old' in 1698 (*OED*),

MEDLEY

A pleasant mistake, madam, that a lady has made, occasions a
little laughter.   50

OLD BELLAIR [to DORIMANT and LADY WOODVILL]

Come, come, you keep 'em idle! They are impatient till the
fiddles play again.

DORIMANT

You are not weary, madam?

LADY WOODVILL

One dance more. I cannot refuse you, Mr Courtage.

They dance. After the dance, OLD BELLAIR *singing and dancing up to*
EMILIA

EMILIA

You are very active, sir.   55

OLD BELLAIR

Adod, sirrah, when I was a young fellow, I could ha' capered up
to my woman's gorget.

DORIMANT [to LADY WOODVILL]

You are willing to rest yourself, madam?

LADY TOWNLEY [to DORIMANT and LADY WOODVILL]

We'll walk into my chamber and sit down.

MEDLEY

Leave us Mr Courtage; he's a dancer, and the young ladies are   60
not weary yet.

LADY WOODVILL

We'll send him out again.

HARRIET

If you do not quickly, I know where to send for Mr Dorimant.

LADY WOODVILL

This girl's head, Mr Courtage, is ever running on that wild
fellow.   65

DORIMANT

'Tis well you have got her a good husband, madam. That will
settle it.

Exeunt LADY TOWNLEY, LADY WOODVILL, *and* DORIMANT

OLD BELLAIR (*to* EMILIA)

Adod, sweetheart, be advised and do not throw thyself away on a
young idle fellow.

EMILIA

I have no such intention, sir.   70

56–7 *capered ... gorget* kicked as high as the garment covering my partner's neck
and shoulders.

OLD BELLAIR

Have a little patience! Thou shalt have the man I spake of. Adod, he loves thee and will make a good husband. But no words—

EMILIA

But, sir—

OLD BELLAIR

No answer—out a pize! Peace, and think on 't.

Enter DORIMANT

DORIMANT

Your company is desired within, sir.   75

OLD BELLAIR

I go, I go! Good Mr Courtage, fare you well. (*To* EMILIA) Go, I'll see you no more!

EMILIA

What have I done, sir?

OLD BELLAIR

You are ugly, you are ugly!—Is she not, Mr Courtage?

EMILIA

Better words, or I shan't abide you!   80

OLD BELLAIR

Out a pize! Adod, what does she say?—Hit her a pat for me there.   *Exit* OLD BELLAIR

MEDLEY [*to* DORIMANT]

You have charms for the whole family.

DORIMANT

You'll spoil all with some unseasonable jest, Medley.

MEDLEY

You see I confine my tongue and am content to be a bare   85
spectator, much contrary to my nature.

EMILIA

Methinks, Mr Dorimant, my Lady Woodvill is a little fond of you.

DORIMANT

Would her daughter were.

MEDLEY

It may be you may find her so. Try her. You have an opportun-   90
ity.

DORIMANT

And I will not lose it. —Bellair, here's a lady has something to say to you.

YOUNG BELLAIR

I wait upon her. —Mr Medley, we have both business with you.

DORIMANT

Get you all together, then. [*He bows to* HARRIET; *she curtsies*] (*To*   95

HARRIET) That demure curtsy is not amiss in jest, but do not
think in earnest it becomes you.
HARRIET
Affectation is catching, I find. From your grave bow I got it.
DORIMANT
Where had you all that scorn and coldness in your look?
HARRIET
From nature, sir—pardon my want of art. I have not learnt those   100
softnesses and languishings which now in faces are so much in
fashion.
DORIMANT
You need 'em not. You have a sweetness of your own, if you
would but calm your frowns and let it settle.
HARRIET
My eyes are wild and wandering like my passions, and cannot yet   105
be tied to rules of charming.
DORIMANT
Women, indeed, have commonly a method of managing those
messengers of love. Now they will look as if they would kill, and
anon they will look as if they were dying. They point and rebate
their glances, the better to invite us.   110
HARRIET
I like this variety well enough, but hate the set face that always
looks as it would say, 'Come love me'—a woman who at plays
makes the *doux yeux* to a whole audience and at home cannot
forbear 'em to her monkey.
DORIMANT
Put on a gentle smile and let me see how well it will become you.   115
HARRIET
I am sorry my face does not please you as it is, but I shall not be
complaisant and change it.
DORIMANT
Though you are obstinate, I know 'tis capable of improvement,
and shall do you justice, madam, if I chance to be at court when
the critics of the circle pass their judgment—for thither you   120
must come.
HARRIET
And expect to be taken in pieces, have all my features examined,

109 *point and rebate* sharpen and blunt
113 *makes ... to* make eyes at

---

117 *complaisant* see note to I, 373.
120 *circle* probably 'an assembly surrounding the principal person' (Johnson), as at
    Court, at a drawing-room or levee, though the *OED*'s first example is from
    1714. More broadly it means a 'set' or coterie.

every motion censured, and on the whole be condemned to be
but pretty—or a beauty of the lowest rate. What think you?
DORIMANT
    The women—nay, the very lovers who belong to the drawing   125
    room—will maliciously allow you more than that. They always
    grant what is apparent, that they may the better be believed
    when they name concealed faults they cannot easily be disproved
    in.
HARRIET
    Beauty runs as great a risk exposed at court as wit does on the   130
    stage, where the ugly and the foolish all are free to censure.
DORIMANT (aside)
    I love her and dare not let her know it. I fear she has an ascendant
    o'er me and may revenge the wrongs I have done her sex. (To her)
    Think of making a party, madam; love will engage.
HARRIET
    You make me start! I did not think to have heard of love from   135
    you.
DORIMANT
    I never knew what 'twas to have a settled ague yet, but now and
    then have had irregular fits.
HARRIET
    Take heed, sickness after long health is commonly more violent
    and dangerous.   140
DORIMANT (aside)
    I have took the infection from her and feel the disease now
    spreading in me. (To her) Is the name of love so frightful that you
    dare not stand it?
HARRIET
    'Twill do little execution out of your mouth on me, I am sure.

132 *ascendant* dominance (orig. astrological)
137 *settled ague* chronic fever

125–6 *drawing room* shortened from 'withdrawing-room', it came to mean a room
    for receptions. From 1673 the word could refer to the people gathered in the
    drawing-room, and hence, a levee, or the sovereign's formal reception at which
    ladies were 'presented' at Court.
130 *risk* as Q1's spelling 'risque' suggests, a relatively recent importation from the
    French. *OED*'s first example dates from 1661.
134 *making a party* 'to make one's party good' means to make good one's cause or
    position; 'to take a party' means making a resolution on one side or the other,
    i.e., Harriet should take the side of beauty against 'the ugly and the foolish' (l.
    131), and love will support her. 'Engage' suggests the possibility of a military
    metaphor—'party' meant a small body of troops selected for a particular duty
    (1645–).

DORIMANT

It has been fatal—   145

HARRIET

To some easy women, but we are not all born to one destiny. I
was informed you use to laugh at love, and not make it.

DORIMANT

The time has been, but now I must speak—

HARRIET

If it be on that idle subject, I will put on my serious look, turn my
head carelessly from you, drop my lip, let my eyelids fall and   150
hang half o'er my eyes—thus, while you buzz a speech of an hour
long in my ear and I answer never a word. Why do you not begin?

DORIMANT

That the company may take notice how passionately I make
advances of love and how disdainfully you receive 'em.

HARRIET

When your love's grown strong enough to make you bear being   155
laughed at, I'll give you leave to trouble me with it. Till when,
pray forbear, sir.

Enter SIR FOPLING *and others in masks*

DORIMANT

What's here—masquerades?

HARRIET

I thought that foppery had been left off, and people might have
been in private with a fiddle.   160

DORIMANT

'Tis endeavoured to be kept on foot still by some who find
themselves the more acceptable the less they are known.

YOUNG BELLAIR

This must be Sir Fopling.

MEDLEY

That extraordinary habit shows it.

YOUNG BELLAIR

What are the rest?   165

147 *use* are accustomed to
164 *habit* dress, attire

153–4 *make advances* the word 'advances' begins to be used in this sense from 1668
  according to the *OED*. For the phrase, compare with French, *faire des avances*.
158 *masquerades* Conaghan aptly cites Burnet, 'At this time [1669] the court fell into
  much extravagance in masquerading; both King and queen, and all the court,
  went about masked, and came into houses unknown, and danced. People were
  so disguised, that without being on the secret none could distinguish them'.
  (*History of my Own Time*, ed. O. Airy (1897), Part I, i, 473.)

MEDLEY

A company of French rascals whom he picked up in Paris and has brought over to be his dancing equipage on these occasions. Make him own himself; a fool is very troublesome when he presumes he is incognito.

SIR FOPLING (*to* HARRIET)

Do you know me?   170

HARRIET

Ten to one but I guess at you.

SIR FOPLING

Are you women as fond of a vizard as we men are?

HARRIET

I am very fond of a vizard that covers a face I do not like, sir.

YOUNG BELLAIR

Here are no masks, you see, sir, but those which came with you. This was intended a private meeting, but because you look like a   175 gentleman, if you will discover yourself and we know you to be such, you shall be welcome.

SIR FOPLING (*pulling off his mask*)

Dear Bellair!

MEDLEY

Sir Fopling! How came you hither?

SIR FOPLING

Faith, as I was coming late from Whitehall, after the King's   180 couchée, one of my people told me he had heard fiddles at my Lady Townley's, and—

DORIMANT

You need not say any more, sir.

SIR FOPLING

Dorimant, let me kiss thee.

DORIMANT

Hark you, Sir Fopling—   *Whispers*   185

SIR FOPLING

Enough, enough, Courtage.—[*Looking at* HARRIET] A pretty kind of young woman that, Medley. I observed her in the Mall,

---

178 s.d. *off* Q3, W, V, B, CA (of Q1)
181 *couchée* ed. (Coucheé Q1; *couchée* V, CA)

---

167 *dancing equipage* see note to III.ii, 166.
180–1 *King's couchée* cf. Fr., *coucher le roi*, the reception preceding the King's going to bed. *OED* cites this as first example in English. Contemporary spelling varies, reflecting its origin. The word was probably brought over by Charles II's Court.

more *éveillée* than our English women commonly are. Prithee, what is she?

MEDLEY

The most noted coquette in town. Beware of her.   190

SIR FOPLING

Let her be what she will, I know how to take my measures. In Paris the mode is to flatter the *prude*, laugh at the *faux-prude*, make serious love to the *demi-prude*, and only rally with the *coquette*. Medley, what think you?

DORIMANT

That for all this smattering of the mathematics, you may be out   195 in your judgment at tennis.

SIR FOPLING

What a *coq-à-l' âne* is this? I talk of women, and thou answerest tennis.

MEDLEY

Mistakes will be, for want of apprehension.

SIR FOPLING

I am very glad of the acquaintance I have with this family.   200

MEDLEY

My lady truly is a good woman.

SIR FOPLING

Ah, Dorimant—Courtage, I would say—would thou hadst spent the last winter in Paris with me. When thou wert there, La

192 *faux-prude* false prude
193 *demi-prude* half prude
193 *with* Q1 (at Q2–3)
197 *coq-à-l'âne* cock and bull story

---

188 *éveillée* wide-awake. Verity cites *Spectator*, No. 45 (21 April 1711), where Addison, advising women to stop their 'Sprightliness from degenerating into Levity', says, 'the whole Discourse and Behaviour of the *French* is to make the Sex more Fantastical, or (as they are pleased to term it,) *more awakened*, than is consistent either with Virtue or Discretion'.

191 *to . . . measures* to make my plans. From the French idiom, *prendre des mesures*, though the first example given by the *OED* is from 1698, indicating that Sir Fopling uses the phrase self-consciously.

191–4 *In Paris . . . coquette* Sir Fopling echoes contemporary French gallantry. See Brett-Smith for a parallel with a poem by Comte de Bussy.

Corneus and Sallyes were the only *habitudes* we had; a comedian
would have been a *bonne fortune*. No stranger ever passed his   205
time so well as I did some months before I came over. I was well
received in a dozen families, where all the women of quality used
to visit. I have intrigues to tell thee more pleasant than ever thou
read'st in a novel.

HARRIET

Write 'em, sir, and oblige us women. Our language wants such   210
little stories.

SIR FOPLING

Writing, madam, 's a mechanic part of wit. A gentleman should
never go beyond a song or a *billet*.

HARRIET

Bussy was a gentleman.

SIR FOPLING

Who, d'Ambois?   215

MEDLEY [*aside*]

Was there ever such a brisk blockhead?

HARRIET

Not d'Ambois, sir, but Rabutin—he who writ the *Loves of
France*.

SIR FOPLING

That may be, madam! Many gentlemen do things that are below

---

208 *to visit* Q1 (to come to visit Q2–3)

---

204 *La Corneus and Sallyes* Verity suggests the fashionable Parisians, Mesdames
Cornuel and Sallé. 'Une certaine madame Sallé, femme d'un maître des com-
ptes' is mentioned in *La France Galante*, often attributed to Comte de Bussy
(see note to IV. i, 217–18) and printed with his *Histoire Amoureuse des Gaulles
(Histoire Amoureuse . . . suivie de la France Galante . . .*, ed. A. Poitevin (Paris,
1857), vol. 2, 355).

204 *habitudes* i.e., acquaintances. *OED* gives this single instance. It may reveal Sir
Fopling's ignorance, or, as Carnochan suggests, come from a memory of the
French idiom, *avoir ses habitudes dans une maison*, to be at home in someone's
house.

204–5 *a comedian . . . fortune* 'The implication is that *even* a comic actor would have
been a "piece of good luck"' (Carnochan). Probably Sir Fopling shows his
ignorance: Madame Cornuel was known for her wit.

215 *d'Ambois* Louis de Clermont d'Amboise, Sieur de Bussy (1549–79), adven-
turer and murderer, familiar to theatregoers as Chapman's *Bussy d'Ambois*
(1607), which was still performed. Sir Fopling's mistake reveals his French
culture as a sham. He knows only the popular Bussy, and not the fashionable
contemporary writer, Comte de Bussy.

217–18 *Rabutin . . . France* Roger de Rabutin, Comte de Bussy (1618–93), author
of the famous *Histoire Amoureuse des Gaulles* and cousin of Madame de Sévigné,
with whom he corresponded. (See also note to l. 204 above.)

'em. —Damn your authors, Courtage, women are the prettiest 220
things we can fool away our time with.

HARRIET

I hope ye have wearied yourself tonight at court, sir, and will not
think of fooling with anybody here.

SIR FOPLING

I cannot complain of my fortune there, madam. —Dorimant—

DORIMANT

Again! 225

SIR FOPLING

Courtage, a pox on 't! I have something to tell thee. When I had
made my court within, I came out and flung myself upon the mat
under the state i' the outward room, i' the midst of half a dozen
beauties who were withdrawn to jeer among themselves, as they
called it. 230

DORIMANT

Did you know 'em?

SIR FOPLING

Not one of 'em, by heavens, not I! But they were all your friends.

DORIMANT

How are you sure of that?

SIR FOPLING

Why, we laughed at all the town—spared nobody but yourself.
They found me a man for their purpose. 235

DORIMANT

I know you are malicious to your power.

SIR FOPLING

And, faith, I had occasion to show it, for I never saw more
gaping fools at a ball or on a Birthday.

DORIMANT

You learned who the women were?

SIR FOPLING

No matter!—they frequent the drawing room. 240

DORIMANT

And entertain themselves pleasantly at the expense of all the fops
who come there.

---

228 *state* canopy
229 *jeer* V, CA (jeèr Q1; jeér W; the accent may, as Carnochan suggests, indicate an
    affected mispronunciation by Sir Fopling)
236 *to your* within your

---

229 *jeer* Carnochan suggests that the early edd. show Sir Fopling using a pseudo-
    French accentuation. But the accenting in Q1 is too eccentric for certainty.
238 *Birthday* celebration of the King's birthday.

SIR FOPLING

That's their business. Faith, I sifted 'em and find they have a sort of wit among them. (*Pinches a tallow candle*)—Ah, filthy!

DORIMANT

Look, he has been pinching the tallow candle. 245

SIR FOPLING

How can you breathe in a room where there's grease frying? Dorimant, thou art intimate with my lady—advise her, for her own sake and the good company that comes hither, to burn wax lights.

HARRIET

What are these masquerades who stand so obsequiously at a 250 distance?

SIR FOPLING

A set of baladines, whom I picked out of the best in France and brought over with a flute douce or two—my servants. They shall entertain you.

HARRIET

I had rather see you dance yourself, Sir Fopling. 255

SIR FOPLING

And I had rather do it—all the company knows it. But, madam—

MEDLEY

Come, come! No excuses, Sir Fopling!

SIR FOPLING

By heavens, Medley—

MEDLEY

Like a woman I find you must be struggled with before one 260 brings you to what you desire.

HARRIET (*aside*)

Can he dance?

EMILIA

And fence and sing too, if you'll believe him.

DORIMANT

He has no more excellence in his heels than in his head. He went

---

243 *sifted* questioned closely, made enquiry of
253 *flute douce* ed. (Flutes deux Q1; Flutes doux CO; *flûtes douces* V; *flûte douce* CA; Q1's 'deux' is probably a misreading of 'doux' in copy)
261 *to* W, V, B, CA, CO (omitted Q1–3)

---

252 *baladines* see note to II.i, 140.
253 *flute douce* see note to II.i, 120.

to Paris a plain, bashful English blockhead, and is returned a   265
fine, undertaking French fop.

MEDLEY [*to* HARRIET]

I cannot prevail.

SIR FOPLING

Do not think it want of complaisance, madam.

HARRIET

You are too well-bred to want that, Sir Fopling. I believe it want
of power.   270

SIR FOPLING

By heavens, and so it is! I have sat up so damned late and drunk
so cursed hard since I came to this lewd town that I am fit for
nothing but low dancing now—a *courante*, a *bourrée*, or a *menuet*.
But St André tells me, if I will but be regular, in one month I
shall rise again. (*Endeavours at a caper*)—Pox on this   275
debauchery!

EMILIA

I have heard your dancing much commended.

SIR FOPLING

It had the good fortune to please in Paris. I was judged to rise
within an inch as high as the Basque in an entry I danced there.

HARRIET [*to* EMILIA]

I am mightily taken with this fool. Let us sit.—Here's a seat, Sir   280
Fopling.

SIR FOPLING

At your feet, madam. I can be nowhere so much at ease.—By
your leave, gown.   [*Sits*]

HARRIET, EMILIA

Ah, you'll spoil it!

SIR FOPLING

No matter, my clothes are my creatures. I make 'em to make my   285

266 *undertaking* possibly chiding, reproving, a sense recorded by *OED* in 1691, or,
    willing to take in hand (i.e. affirmative and positive where he had once been
    'plain and bashful').

273 *low dancing . . . menuet* the three dances are 'low' because they call for no
    'capers'.

274 *St André* a French dancer brought over to perform in Shadwell's *Psyche* (1675)
    and described as 'the most famous Master of *France*' (Preface). He also heads
    the list of dancers in Crowne's *Calisto*, produced at Court in the same year.

279 *the Basque* probably a reference to 'le Basque sauteur', a French dancer whose
    affair with Madame de Berthillac is recounted in *La France Galante* (ed.
    Poitevin, vol. 2, 84–5).

279 *entry* a dance introduced between the parts of an entertainment. A fairly new
    word (from Fr. *entrée* or *entrée de ballet*). *OED*'s earliest example dates from
    1651, 'A masque at Court, where the French King in person danced five
    entries' (Evelyn, *Memoirs* (1857), vol. 1, 276).

court to you ladies.—Hey! *qu'on commence*!   *Dance*
(*To* [JOHN TROTT, *one of the dancers*])—English motions! I was
forced to entertain this fellow, one of my set miscarrying.—Oh,
horrid! Leave your damned manner of dancing and put on the
French air. Have you not a pattern before you?   290
[*Dances*]—Pretty well! Imitation in time may bring him to
something.

After the dance, enter OLD BELLAIR, LADY WOODVILL, *and* LADY
TOWNLEY

OLD BELLAIR
Hey, adod, what have we here? A mumming?
LADY WOODVILL
Where's my daughter?—Harriet!
DORIMANT
Here, here, madam. I know not but under these disguises there   295
may be dangerous sparks. I gave the young lady warning.
LADY WOODVILL
Lord! I am so obliged to you Mr Courtage.
HARRIET
Lord! How you admire this man!
LADY WOODVILL
What have you to except against him?
HARRIET
He's a fop.   300
LADY WOODVILL
He's not a Dorimant, a wild, extravagant fellow of the times.

---

286 *qu'on commence* begin!
286–7 *commence*! ... *motions*! ed. (Comencé, English motions. Q1ᵘ; Comencé to an
       English Dancer English motions Q1ᶜ; *commence*—to an English dancer
       English motions. V, B, CA (who further adds an s.d. after 'fellow' in l. 288,
       '*pointing to John Trott*'); CO first introduced the emendation
288 *entertain* retain, hire
288 *miscarrying* coming to harm, or behaving badly, or going astray
290 *not a* Q1ᶜ (not had a Q1ᵘ)

286–7 *commence*! ... *motions*! Conaghan, who first discovered the corrected and
       uncorrected states, gives 'to an English Dancer' as an s.d., and comments,
       'Lack of punctuation in Q1ᶜ suggests that the compositor made the insertion
       without attending to its purpose: *to ... Dancer* is almost certainly a stage
       direction'. Q1's reading makes possible sense as Sir Fopling's interjection, but
       Conaghan's emendation is preferable.
290 *not a* as Conaghan says, the change in Q1ᶜ 'allows for a demonstration of
       dancing by Sir Fopling'.
301 *wild, extravagant* see Introduction, pp. xxix–xxxiii.

HARRIET

    He's a man made up of forms and commonplaces, sucked out of
    the remaining lees of the last age.

LADY WOODVILL

    He's so good a man that were you not engaged—

LADY TOWNLEY

    You'll have but little night to sleep in.   305

LADY WOODVILL

    Lord! 'tis perfect day—

DORIMANT (*aside*)

    The hour is almost come I appointed Bellinda, and I am not so
    foppishly in love here to forget. I am flesh and blood yet.

LADY TOWNLEY

    I am very sensible, madam.

LADY WOODVILL

    Lord, madam—   310

HARRIET

    Look, in what a struggle is my poor mother yonder!

YOUNG BELLAIR

    She has much ado to bring out the compliment.

DORIMANT

    She strains hard for it.

HARRIET

    See, see—her head tottering, her eyes staring, and her underlip
    trembling.   315

DORIMANT

    Now, now she's in the very convulsions of her civility.
    (*Aside*)—'Sdeath, I shall lose Bellinda! I must fright her hence.
    She'll be an hour in this fit of good manners else. (*To* LADY
    WOODVILL) Do you not know Sir Fopling, madam?

LADY WOODVILL

    I have seen that face. Oh heaven!—'tis the same we met in the   320
    Mall! How came he here?

DORIMANT

    A fiddle in this town is a kind of fop-call. No sooner it strikes up,
    but the house is besieged with an army of masquerades straight.

LADY WOODVILL

    Lord, I tremble, Mr Courtage! For certain Dorimant is in the
    company.   325

DORIMANT

    I cannot confidently say he is not. You had best begone; I will
    wait upon you. Your daughter is in the hands of Mr Bellair.

302 *forms* see note to I, 110–11.

306 *perfect day* i.e., broad daylight

309 *sensible* aware of (your courtesy)

LADY WOODVILL

I'll see her before me.—Harriet, come away!

                       [*Exeunt* LADY WOODVILL *and* HARRIET]

YOUNG BELLAIR

Lights, lights!

LADY TOWNLEY

Light, down there!   330

OLD BELLAIR

Adod, it needs not—

        [*Exeunt* LADY TOWNLEY, EMILIA *and* YOUNG BELLAIR]

DORIMANT [*calling to the servants outside*]

Call my Lady Woodvill's coach to the door, quickly.

                                 [*Exit* DORIMANT]

OLD BELLAIR

Stay, Mr Medley, let the young fellows do that duty. We will drink a glass of wine together. 'Tis good after dancing. [*Looks at* SIR FOPLING]—What mumming spark is that?   335

MEDLEY

He is not to be comprehended in few words.

SIR FOPLING

Hey, La Tour!

MEDLEY

Whither away, Sir Fopling?

SIR FOPLING

I have business with Courtage.

MEDLEY

He'll but put the ladies into their coach and come up again.   340

OLD BELLAIR

In the meantime I'll call for a bottle.   [*Exit* OLD BELLAIR]

Enter YOUNG BELLAIR

MEDLEY

Where's Dorimant?

YOUNG BELLAIR

Stolen home. He has had business waiting for him there all this night, I believe, by an impatience I observed in him.

MEDLEY

Very likely. 'Tis but dissembling drunkenness, railing at his   345 friends, and the kind soul will embrace the blessing and forget the tedious expectation.

SIR FOPLING

I must speak with him before I sleep.

YOUNG BELLAIR [*to* MEDLEY]

Emilia and I are resolved on that business.

337 *Tour* V, CA (Towèr Q1)

MEDLEY
   Peace, here's your father.   350

    Enter OLD BELLAIR *and butler with a bottle of wine*

OLD BELLAIR
   The women are all gone to bed.—Fill, boy!—Mr Medley, begin
   a health.
MEDLEY (*whispers*)
   To Emilia.
OLD BELLAIR
   Out a pize! She's a rogue, and I'll not pledge you.
MEDLEY
   I know you will.   355
OLD BELLAIR
   Adod, drink it, then!
SIR FOPLING
   Let us have the new *bachique*.
OLD BELLAIR
   Adod, that is a hard word! What does it mean, sir?
MEDLEY
   A catch or drinking song.
OLD BELLAIR
   Let us have it, then.   360
SIR FOPLING
   Fill the glasses round, and draw up in a body.—Hey, music!

                They sing

   The pleasures of love and the joys of good wine,
   To perfect our happiness wisely we join.
     We to beauty all day
     Give the sovereign sway   365
   And her favourite nymphs devoutly obey.
   At the plays we are constantly making our court,

355 *will* V, B, CA (well Q1)

---

357 *bachique* drinking song, as Medley explains. *OED* cites this as its single
   example (cf. Fr. *chanson bachique*). Although it occurs as an adjective from 1669
   to 1699, this is probably another example of Sir Fopling's French, not the
   isolated occurrence of an English word.
362–83 *The pleasures ... fire* Thorpe, p. 103, records several subsequent printed
   appearances of this song, and notes Etherege's own preference for women over
   heavy drinking; as Dryden said, 'For wine to leave a whore or play/Was ne'er
   Your Excellence's way' ('Mr Dryden's Letter to Sir George Etherege', ll.
   53–4). Carnochan cites lines from two songs in Shadwell's *Psyche* (1675) which
   deal with the *topoi* of the first two lines of Etherege's song.

And when they are ended, we follow the sport
   To the Mall and the Park,
   Where we love till 'tis dark.   370
   Then sparkling champagne
   Puts an end to their reign:
   It quickly recovers
   Poor languishing lovers,
Makes us frolic and gay, and drowns all our sorrow;   375
But alas, we relapse again on the morrow.
   Let every man stand
   With his glass in his hand,
And briskly discharge at the word of command.
   Here's a health to all those   380
   Whom tonight we depose.
Wine and beauty by turns great souls should inspire;
Present all together—and now, boys, give fire!

[They drink]

OLD BELLAIR
   Adod, a pretty business and very merry!
SIR FOPLING
   Hark you, Medley, let you and I take the fiddles and go waken   385
   Dorimant.
MEDLEY
   We shall do him a courtesy, if it be as I guess. For after the
   fatigue of this night, he'll quickly have his belly full and be glad
   of an occasion to cry, 'Take away, Handy!'
YOUNG BELLAIR
   I'll go with you; and there we'll consult about affairs, Medley.   390
OLD BELLAIR
   Adod, 'tis six o'clock!
SIR FOPLING
   Let's away, then.
OLD BELLAIR
   Mr Medley, my sister tells me you are an honest man. And,

---

382 *should* Q1 (*shall* Q2–3)

371 *champagne* a new word (and drink) from the French. First example in *OED* is
   from *Hudibras* (1664). The modern technique for making champagne is the
   invention of Dom Pérignon, cellarer at the Abbey of Hautvillers from 1668 to
   1715, though champagne was available prior to his discoveries.
383 *Present all together* i.e., raise your drinks and aim. The military metaphor runs
   through the song's last seven lines.

adod, I love you.—Few words and hearty, that's the way with
old Harry, old Harry.   395

SIR FOPLING [*to his servants*]

Light your flambeaux! Hey!

OLD BELLAIR

What does the man mean?

MEDLEY

'Tis day, Sir Fopling.

SIR FOPLING

No matter; our serenade will look the greater.   *Exeunt omnes*

Act IV, Scene ii

DORIMANT's *lodging; a table, a candle, a toilet, etc.* HANDY *tying up
linen*

Enter DORIMANT *in his gown, and* BELLINDA

DORIMANT

Why will you be gone so soon?

BELLINDA

Why did you stay out so late?

DORIMANT

Call a chair, Handy.   [*Exit* HANDY]
—What makes you tremble so?

BELLINDA

I have a thousand fears about me. Have I not been seen, think   5
you?

DORIMANT

By nobody but myself and trusty Handy.

BELLINDA

Where are all your people?

DORIMANT

I have dispersed 'em on sleeveless errands. What does that sigh
mean?   10

BELLINDA

Can you be so unkind to ask me? Well—(*sighs*)—were it to do
again—

DORIMANT

We should do it, should we not?

BELLINDA

I think we should: the wickeder man you, to make me love so
well. Will you be discreet now?   15

396 *flambeaux* torches, esp. ones made from several thick wicks dipped in wax
  9 *sleeveless* trifling

399 *serenade* see note to II.i, 115.

DORIMANT
  I will.

BELLINDA
  You cannot.

DORIMANT
  Never doubt it.

BELLINDA
  I will not expect it.

DORIMANT
  You do me wrong.   20

BELLINDA
  You have no more power to keep the secret than I had not to trust
  you with it.

DORIMANT
  By all the joys I have had, and those you keep in store—

BELLINDA
  —You'll do for my sake what you never did before.

DORIMANT
  By that truth thou hast spoken, a wife shall sooner betray herself   25
  to her husband.

BELLINDA
  Yet I had rather you should be false in this than in another thing
  you promised me.

DORIMANT
  What's that?

BELLINDA
  That you would never see Loveit more but in public places—in   30
  the Park, at court and plays.

DORIMANT
  'Tis not likely a man should be fond of seeing a damned old play
  when there is a new one acted.

BELLINDA
  I dare not trust your promise.

DORIMANT
  You may.   35

BELLINDA
  This does not satisfy me. You shall swear you never will see her
  more.

DORIMANT
  I will, a thousand oaths! By all—

BELLINDA
  Hold! You shall not, now I think on 't better.

23–4 *By ... before* Dorimant's speech begins to fall into an Alexandrine, but
    Bellinda 'is quick to interrupt his heroics with her rhyming reply' (Brett-
    Smith).

DORIMANT
I will swear!   40
BELLINDA
I shall grow jealous of the oath and think I owe your truth to that,
not to your love.
DORIMANT
Then, by my love! No other oath I'll swear.

Enter HANDY

HANDY
Here's a chair.
BELLINDA
Let me go.   45
DORIMANT
I cannot.
BELLINDA
Too willingly, I fear.
DORIMANT
Too unkindly feared. When will you promise me again?
BELLINDA
Not this fortnight.
DORIMANT
You will be better than your word.   50
BELLINDA
I think I shall. Will it not make you love me less?
                                        Fiddles without
(*Starting*) Hark, what fiddles are these?
DORIMANT
Look out, Handy.   *Exit* HANDY *and returns*
HANDY
Mr Medley, Mr Bellair, and Sir Fopling. They are coming up.
DORIMANT
How got they in?   55
HANDY
The door was open for the chair.
BELLINDA
Lord, let me fly!
DORIMANT
Here, here, down the back stairs. I'll see you into your chair.
BELLINDA
No, no! Stay and receive 'em. And be sure you keep your word
and never see Loveit more. Let it be a proof of your kindness.   60
DORIMANT
It shall.—Handy, direct her.—(*Kissing her hand*) Everlasting

love go along with thee.   *Exeunt* BELLINDA *and* HANDY

Enter YOUNG BELLAIR, MEDLEY, *and* SIR FOPLING [*with his page*]

YOUNG BELLAIR
Not abed yet?
MEDLEY
You have had an irregular fit, Dorimant.
DORIMANT
I have.   65
YOUNG BELLAIR
And is it off already?
DORIMANT
Nature has done her part, gentlemen. When she falls kindly to
work, great cures are effected in little time, you know.
SIR FOPLING
We thought there was a wench in the case, by the chair that
waited. Prithee, make us a *confidence*.   70
DORIMANT
Excuse me.
SIR FOPLING
Le sage Dorimant. Was she pretty?
DORIMANT
So pretty she may come to keep her coach and pay parish duties,
if the good humour of the age continue.
MEDLEY
And be of the number of the ladies kept by public-spirited men   75
for the good of the whole town.
SIR FOPLING
Well said, Medley.   SIR FOPLING *dancing by himself*
YOUNG BELLAIR
See Sir Fopling dancing.
DORIMANT
You are practising and have a mind to recover, I see.
SIR FOPLING
Prithee, Dorimant, why hast not thou a glass hung up here? A   80
room is the dullest thing without one!
YOUNG BELLAIR
Here is company to entertain you.

---

72 *Le sage* judicious, discreet

---

64 *irregular fit* unexpected bout of illness. Presumably Medley overhears Dorim-
    ant at IV.i, 138.
73–4 *So ... continue* 'an instance of Dorimant's discretion. The description could
    hardly apply to Bellinda, who is not mercenary' (Conaghan).

SIR FOPLING
But I mean in case of being alone. In a glass a man may entertain
himself—

DORIMANT
The shadow of himself, indeed.   85

SIR FOPLING
—Correct the errors of his motions and his dress.

MEDLEY
I find, Sir Fopling, in your solitude you remember the saying of
the wise man, and study yourself.

SIR FOPLING
'Tis the best diversion in our retirements. Dorimant, thou art a
pretty fellow and wearest thy clothes well, but I never saw thee   90
have a handsome cravat. Were they made up like mine, they'd
give another air to thy face. Prithee, let me send my man to dress
thee but one day. By heavens, an Englishman cannot tie a
ribbon!

DORIMANT
They are something clumsy-fisted.   95

SIR FOPLING
I have brought over the prettiest fellow that ever spread a toilet.
He served some time under Mérille, the greatest *génie* in the
world for a *valet de chambre*.

DORIMANT
What, he who formerly belonged to the Duke of Candale?

SIR FOPLING
The same, and got him his immortal reputation.   100

---

97 *Mérille* Mérille had been in service with the Duc de Candale, and was his
'principal confident'. After de Candale's death Mérille was in service with the
Duc d'Orléans and by 1673 was his 'premier valet de chambre' (*Correspondance*
(1858), vol. 3, 240).

97 *génie* man of genius (cf. Fr. *homme de génie*). *OED* gives only three instances, of
which this is the first, between 1676 and 1687. It should probably be regarded
as a French word.

98 *valet de chambre* although *OED* records this as English from 1646 onwards, and
Handy is so described in the Dramatis Personæ, Sir Fopling looks to the
French (as Q1's spelling, 'Valet d'Chambré', may indicate).

99 *Duke of Candale* Louis-Charles Gaston de Nogaret de Foix, Duc de Candale
(1627–58), French general. Bussy reports, 'Sa taille étoit admirable. Il s'habil-
loit bien, et les plus proches tâchoient de l'imiter', but attributed this not to his
valet but his mistress: Mlle de la Roche-Posay 'avoit pris tant de soin de le
dresser, et lui de plaire cette belle, que l'art avoit passé le nature, et qu'il étoit
beaucoup plus honnête homme que mille gens qui avoient plus d'esprit que lui'
(*Histoire Amoureuse . . .*, ed. Poitevin (1857), vol. 1, 69–70).

DORIMANT
    You've a very fine brandenburgh on, Sir Fopling.
SIR FOPLING
    It serves to wrap me up, after the fatigue of a ball.
MEDLEY
    I see you often in it, with your periwig tied up.
SIR FOPLING
    We should not always be in a set dress. 'Tis more *en cavalier* to
    appear now and then in a *déshabillé*.   105
MEDLEY
    Pray, how goes your business with Loveit?
SIR FOPLING
    You might have answered yourself in the Mall last
    night.—Dorimant, did you not see the advances she made me? I
    have been endeavouring at a song.
DORIMANT
    Already?   110
SIR FOPLING
    'Tis my *coup d'essai* in English. I would fain have thy opinion of
    it.
DORIMANT
    Let's see it.
SIR FOPLING
    Hey, page, give me my song.—Bellair, here. Thou hast a pretty
    voice, sing it.   115
YOUNG BELLAIR
    Sing it yourself, Sir Fopling.
SIR FOPLING
    Excuse me.
YOUNG BELLAIR
    You learnt to sing in Paris.

---

104 *en cavalier* jaunty, dashing
105 *déshabillé* V, CA (dissabillé Q1)
111 *coup d'essai* trial shot, first attempt

---

101 *brandenburgh* morning gown (named after the Prussian city famous for its
    woollen goods). Conaghan cites the epilogue to Lee's *Gloriana* (1676): 'Huge
    Brandenburgh had so disguis'd each one,/That from your Coachman you could
    scarce be known'. *OED* cites Etherege's use as its first occurrence, but there is
    an earlier instance in Wycherley's *The Plain-Dealer* (1677, first acted 1674).
103 *periwig tied up* i.e., to save combing.
105 *in a déshabillé* casually dressed, Q1's spelling, 'dissabilée', appears to be a
    phonetic rendering of the French. Compare with II.ii, 76 and textual note. The
    audience may have felt a pun.
108 *advances ... made* see not to IV.i, 153–4.

SIR FOPLING

I did—of Lambert, the greatest master in the world; but I have
his own fault, a weak voice, and care not to sing out of a ruelle.   120

DORIMANT

A ruelle is a pretty cage for a singing fop, indeed.

                                          YOUNG BELLAIR *reads the song*

    How charming Phillis is, how fair!
      Ah, that she were as willing
    To ease my wounded heart of care,
      And make her eyes less killing.   125
    I sigh! I sigh! I languish now,
      And love will not let me rest;
    I drive about the Park and bow,
      Still as I meet my dearest.

SIR FOPLING

Sing it, sing it, man! It goes to a pretty new tune which I am   130
confident was made by Baptiste.

MEDLEY

Sing it yourself, Sir Fopling. He does not know the tune.

SIR FOPLING

I'll venture.   SIR FOPLING *sings*

DORIMANT

Ay, marry, now 'tis something. I shall not flatter you, Sir
Fopling: there is not much thought in 't, but 'tis passionate and   135
well-turned.

129 *Still as* whenever

---

119 *Lambert* Michel Lambert (1610–96), French lutenist and singer. He was made
master of the royal chamber music by Cardinal Richelieu, and was a popular
teacher in Louis XIV's Court.

120, 121 *ruelle* 'a bedroom, where ladies of fashion, in the seventeenth and
eighteenth centuries, esp. in France, held a morning reception of persons of
distinction; hence, a reception of this kind' (*OED*, which gives this as its first
example). As Brett-Smith points out, Littré's *Dictionnaire* (1863–72) shows the
peculiar aptness to Sir Fopling better—'se disait particulièrement des
chambres à coucher sous Louis XIV, des alcôves de certaines dames de qualité,
servant de salon de conversation et où régnait souvent le ton précieux'.

122–9 *How ... dearest* Thorpe (p. 104) gives later printings, those from 1707
onwards having music by Ramonden, though its satirical intent is lost out of
context in the songbooks.

131 *Baptiste* probably Jean-Baptiste Lully (1632–87), Louis XIV's master of court
music, composer, and credited with the founding of French opera. Called by
Pepys (18 June 1666) 'the present great composer'. But, as Conaghan says,
'Baptist' at this time often refers to Giovanni Battista Draghi (*c.* 1640–*c.* 1710),
an Italian harpsichordist and composer, who had settled in England after the
Restoration. He composed the operatic music for Shadwell's adaptation of *The
Tempest* (1674) as well as for his *Psyche* (1675).

MEDLEY

After the French way.

SIR FOPLING

That I aimed at. Does it not give you a lively image of the thing?
Slap, down goes the glass, and thus we are at it.

DORIMANT

It does indeed. I perceive, Sir Fopling, you'll be the very head of 140
the sparks who are lucky in compositions of this nature.

Enter SIR FOPLING'S FOOTMAN

SIR FOPLING

La Tour, is the bath ready?

FOOTMAN

Yes, sir.

SIR FOPLING

Adieu donc, mes chers.

Exit SIR FOPLING [*with* FOOTMAN *and* PAGE]

MEDLEY

When have you your revenge on Loveit, Dorimant?   145

DORIMANT

I will but change my linen and about it.

MEDLEY

The powerful considerations which hindered have been
removed then?

DORIMANT

Most luckily, this morning. You must go along with me; my
reputation lies at stake there.   150

MEDLEY

I am engaged to Bellair.

DORIMANT

What's your business?

MEDLEY

Ma-tri-mony, an't like you.

DORIMANT

It does not, sir.

YOUNG BELLAIR

It may in time, Dorimant. What think you of Mrs Harriet?   155

142 *Tour* V, CA (Tower Q1)
144 *Adieu donc, mes chers* goodbye then, my friends

139 *glass* Carnochan suggests 'coach-window', but looking-glass seems more likely
    from the context.
153 *Ma-tri-mony an't like you* i.e., 'Medley mimics tradesmen's speech, in response
    to Dorimant's "business"' (Conaghan).

DORIMANT

What does she think of me?

YOUNG BELLAIR

I am confident she loves you.

DORIMANT

How does it appear?

YOUNG BELLAIR

Why, she's never well but when she's talking of you, but then she
finds all the faults in you she can. She laughs at all who commend   160
you; but then she speaks ill of all who do not.

DORIMANT

Women of her temper betray themselves by their over-cunning.
I had once a growing love with a lady who would always quarrel
with me when I came to see her, and yet was never quiet if I
stayed a day from her.   165

YOUNG BELLAIR

My father is in love with Emilia.

DORIMANT

That is a good warrant for your proceedings. Go on and
prosper—I must to Loveit. Medley, I am sorry you cannot be a
witness.

MEDLEY

Make her meet Sir Fopling again in the same place and use him   170
ill before me.

DORIMANT

That may be brought about, I think.—I'll be at your aunt's anon
and give you joy, Mr Bellair.

YOUNG BELLAIR

You had not best think of Mrs Harriet too much. Without
church security, there's no taking up there.   175

DORIMANT

I may fall into the snare, too. But,
    The wise will find a difference in our fate:
    You wed a woman, I a good estate.   *Exeunt*

---

173 *give you joy* congratulate you
174 *not best* Q1 (best not CA)

---

175 *taking up* hire, buy up wholesale, borrow at interest (extending the metaphor
established in 'church security').

Act IV, Scene iii
[*Outside* MRS LOVEIT'*s*]

Enter the chair with BELLINDA; *the men set it down and open it.*
BELLINDA *starting*

BELLINDA (*surprised*)
Lord, where am I? In the Mall! Whither have you brought me?

FIRST CHAIRMAN
You gave us no directions, madam.

BELLINDA (*aside*)
The fright I was in made me forget it.

FIRST CHAIRMAN
We use to carry a lady from the squire's hither.

BELLINDA (*aside*)
This is Loveit! I am undone if she sees me.—Quickly, carry me   5
away!

FIRST CHAIRMAN
Whither, an't like your honour?

BELLINDA
Ask no questions!

Enter Mrs Loveit's FOOTMAN

FOOTMAN
Have you seen my lady, madam?

BELLINDA
I am just come to wait upon her.   10

FOOTMAN
She will be glad to see you, madam. She sent me to you this
morning to desire your company, and I was told you went out by
five o'clock.

BELLINDA (*aside*)
More and more unlucky!

FOOTMAN
Will you walk in, madam?   15

BELLINDA
I'll discharge my chair and follow. Tell your mistress I am here.
[*Exit* FOOTMAN]
Take this!([BELLINDA] *gives the* CHAIRMEN *money*)—and if ever
you should be examined, be sure you say you took me up in the
Strand, over against the Exchange—as you will answer it to Mr
Dorimant.

CHAIRMEN

We will, an't like your honour.   [*Exeunt* CHAIRMEN]   20

BELLINDA

Now to come off, I must on:
    In confidence and lies some hope is left;
        'Twere hard to be found out in the first theft.   *Exit*

Act V, Scene i
[MRS LOVEIT'S]

Enter MRS LOVEIT *and* PERT, *her woman*

PERT
  Well! In my eyes, Sir Fopling is no such despicable person.
MRS LOVEIT
  You are an excellent judge.
PERT
  He's as handsome a man as Mr Dorimant, and as great a gallant.
MRS LOVEIT
  Intolerable! Is 't not enough I submit to his impertinences, but
  must I be plagued with yours too?   5
PERT
  Indeed, madam—
MRS LOVEIT
  'Tis false, mercenary malice—

Enter her FOOTMAN

FOOTMAN
  Mrs Bellinda, madam.
MRS LOVEIT
  What of her?
FOOTMAN
  She's below.   10
MRS LOVEIT
  How came she?
FOOTMAN
  In a chair—Ambling Harry brought her.
MRS LOVEIT
  He bring her! His chair stands near Dorimant's door and always
  brings me from thence.—Run and ask him where he took her
  up. Go!   [*Exit* FOOTMAN]   15
  There is no truth in friendship neither. Women as well as men,
  all are false—or all are so to me at least.
PERT
  You are jealous of her too?
MRS LOVEIT
  You had best tell her I am. 'Twill become the liberty you take of
  late. [*Aside*] This fellow's bringing of her, her going out by five   20
  o'clock—I know not what to think.

Enter BELLINDA

Bellinda, you are grown an early riser, I hear!

BELLINDA

Do you not wonder, my dear, what made me abroad so soon?

MRS LOVEIT

You do not use to be so.

BELLINDA

The country gentlewomen I told you of—Lord, they have the   25
oddest diversions!—would never let me rest till I promised to go
with them to the markets this morning to eat fruit and buy
nosegays.

MRS LOVEIT

Are they so fond of a filthy nosegay?

BELLINDA

They complain of the stinks of the town and are never well but   30
when they have their noses in one.

MRS LOVEIT

There are essences and sweet waters.

BELLINDA

Oh, they cry out upon perfumes, they are unwholesome. One of
'em was falling into a fit with the smell of these nerolii.

MRS LOVEIT

Methinks, in complaisance you should have had a nosegay too.   35

BELLINDA

Do you think, my dear, I could be so loathsome to trick myself
up with carnations and stock-gillyflowers? I begged their pardon
and told them I never wore anything but orange-flowers and
tuberose. That which made me willing to go was a strange desire
I had to eat some fresh nectarines.   40

MRS LOVEIT

And had you any?

34 *nerolii* presumably the plural of 'neroli', which normally meant the essential oil
   distilled from the flowers of the bitter orange and used for scenting gloves.
   (Named after the Italian princess to whom its discovery is attributed.) Here it
   seems to refer to the gloves worn by Bellinda (see l. 38). For the popularity of
   essence of orange, see note to III.ii, 207.
35 *complaisance* see note to I, 373.
37 *stock-gillyflower* white stock (*matthiola incana*). So-called both because of its
   clove-like smell and because it blooms in July.
39 *tuberose* liliaceous flower, with creamy white, funnel-shaped, fragrant flowers
   and a tuberous root. Like the orange-flower this was an exotic having only
   recently reached England (Evelyn mentions it in 1664 and the *London Gazette*,
   No. 2654/4 (1691), reports, 'There are lately brought from Italy . . . Onions of
   Tubereuse'). In the language of flowers, tuberose signifies dangerous
   pleasures.

BELLINDA

The best I ever tasted.

MRS LOVEIT

Whence came you now?

BELLINDA

From their lodgings, where I crowded out of a coach and took a
chair to come and see you, my dear.   4!

MRS LOVEIT

Whither did you send for that chair?

BELLINDA

'Twas going by empty.

MRS LOVEIT

Where do these country gentlewomen lodge, I pray?

BELLINDA

In the Strand, over against the Exchange.

PERT

That place is never without a nest of 'em. They are always, as one   50
goes by, fleering in balconies or staring out of windows.

Enter FOOTMAN

MRS LOVEIT (*to the* FOOTMAN)

Come hither.   *Whispers*

BELLINDA (*aside*)

This fellow by her order has been questioning the chairmen. I
threatened 'em with the name of Dorimant. If they should have
told truth, I am lost forever.   55

MRS LOVEIT

In the Strand, said you?

FOOTMAN

Yes, madam, over against the Exchange.   [*Exit* FOOTMAN]

MRS LOVEIT

She's innocent, and I am much to blame.

BELLINDA (*aside*)

I am so frightened my countenance will betray me.

MRS LOVEIT

Bellinda, what makes you look so pale?   60

BELLINDA

Want of my usual rest and jolting up and down so long in an
odious hackney.

FOOTMAN *returns*

51 *fleering* jeering

48–51 *Where ... windows* see note to I, 54.

FOOTMAN

Madam, Mr Dorimant.   [*Exit* FOOTMAN]

MRS LOVEIT

What makes him here?

BELLINDA (*aside*)

Then I am betrayed indeed. He has broke his word, and I love a   65
man that does not care for me.

MRS LOVEIT

Lord!—you faint, Bellinda.

BELLINDA

I think I shall—such an oppression here on the sudden.

PERT

She has eaten too much fruit, I warrant you.

MRS LOVEIT

Not unlikely.   70

PERT

'Tis that lies heavy on her stomach.

MRS LOVEIT

Have her into my chamber, give her some surfeit-water, and let
her lie down a little.

PERT

Come, madam. I was a strange devourer of fruit when I was
young—so ravenous.   75

              Exeunt BELLINDA *and* PERT, *leading her off*

MRS LOVEIT

Oh, that my love would be but calm awhile, that I might receive
this man with all the scorn and indignation he deserves!

                      Enter DORIMANT

DORIMANT

Now for a touch of Sir Fopling to begin with.—Hey, page! Give
positive order that none of my people stir. Let the *canaille* wait,
as they should do.—Since noise and nonsense have such   80
powerful charms,

              'I, that I may successful prove,
              Transform myself to what you love'.

---

64 *What ... here* What's brought him here?
72 *surfeit-water* medicinal drink made by diffusion or distillation
74 *strange* exceptional
79 *canaille* riff-raff

82–3 *I ... love* Waller, 'To the Mutable Fair', ll. 5–6 (*Poems*, ed. G. Thorn Drury
   (1901), vol. 1, 106). Dorimant changes the first word from 'And' to 'I'.

MRS LOVEIT

If that would do, you need not change from what you are—you
can be vain and loud enough.   85

DORIMANT

But not with so good a grace as Sir Fopling.—'Hey, Hampshire!'—Oh, that sound! That sound becomes the mouth of a
man of quality.

MRS LOVEIT

Is there a thing so hateful as a senseless mimic?

DORIMANT

He's a great grievance, indeed, to all who—like yourself,   90
madam—love to play the fool in quiet.

MRS LOVEIT

A ridiculous animal, who has more of the ape than the ape has of
the man in him.

DORIMANT

I have as mean an opinion of a sheer mimic as yourself; yet were
he all ape, I should prefer him to the gay, the giddy, brisk,   95
insipid, noisy fool you dote on.

MRS LOVEIT

Those noisy fools, however you despise 'em, have good qualities
which weigh more (or ought, at least) with us women than all the
pernicious wit you have to boast of.

DORIMANT

That I may hereafter have a just value for their merit, pray do me 100
the favour to name 'em.

MRS LOVEIT

You'll despise 'em as the dull effects of ignorance and vanity, yet
I care not if I mention some. First, they really admire us, while
you at best but flatter us well.

DORIMANT

Take heed!—fools can dissemble too.   105

MRS LOVEIT

They may—but not so artificially as you. There is no fear they
should deceive us. Then, they are assiduous, sir. They are ever
offering us their service and always waiting on our will.

DORIMANT

You owe that to their excessive idleness. They know not how to
entertain themselves at home, and find so little welcome abroad, 110
they are fain to fly to you who countenance 'em, as a refuge
against the solitude they would be otherwise condemned to.

MRS LOVEIT

Their conversation, too, diverts us better.

DORIMANT

Playing with your fan, smelling to your gloves, commending

your hair, and taking notice how 'tis cut and shaded after the new   115
way—

MRS LOVEIT

Were it sillier than you can make it, you must allow 'tis pleasanter
to laugh at others than to be laughed at ourselves, though never
so wittily. Then, though they want skill to flatter us, they flatter
themselves so well, they save us the labour. We need not take   120
that care and pains to satisfy 'em of our love, which we so often
lose on you.

DORIMANT

They commonly, indeed, believe too well of themselves, and
always better of you than you deserve.

MRS LOVEIT

You are in the right: they have an implicit faith in us, which   125
keeps 'em from prying narrowly into our secrets, and saves us the
vexatious trouble of clearing doubts which your subtle and
causeless jealousies every moment raise.

DORIMANT

There is an inbred falsehood in women which inclines 'em still to
them whom they may most easily deceive.   130

MRS LOVEIT

The man who loves above his quality does not suffer more from
the insolent impertinence of his mistress than the woman who
loves above her understanding does from the arrogant presump-
tions of her friend.

DORIMANT

You mistake the use of fools: they are designed for properties   135
and not for friends. You have an indifferent stock of reputation
left yet. Lose it all like a frank gamester on the square. 'Twill
then be time enough to turn rook and cheat it up again on a good,
substantial bubble.

135 *properties* mere instruments, tools, cat's-paws
136 *indifferent* tolerable
138 *rook* cheat, swindler (especially in gaming)

---

137 *on the square* face to face, openly. The modern idiom makes sense here, and was
    in use from 1611, but the phrase may have been a term in gaming. The sense,
    'without deceit, fraud, or trickery' occurs from 1667–68 onwards, and is
    frequently used of gaming. Wheadle, the gamester in *Love in a Tub*, says that he
    could stay within the law if he could give up gaming—'Could I but leave this
    Ordinary [notorious for late-night gaming], this Square . . .' (I.ii). Brett-Smith
    is unable to explain this, but taking the two passages together the 'square' may
    refer to the gaming-table or board.
139 *bubble* a dupe or gull, esp. in gaming. A Restoration word. The use of the verb
    by Wheadle in *Love in a Tub* (1664), II.iii, precedes the first instance in *OED*,
    and suggests that it began as gaming slang.

MRS LOVEIT

The old and the ill-favoured are only fit for properties, indeed,   140
but young and handsome fools have met with kinder fortunes.

DORIMANT

They have, to the shame of your sex be it spoken. 'Twas this, the
thought of this, made me by a timely jealousy endeavour to
prevent the good fortune you are providing for Sir Fopling. But
against a woman's frailty all our care is vain.   145

MRS LOVEIT

Had I not with a dear experience bought the knowledge of your
falsehood, you might have fooled me yet. This is not the first
jealousy you have feigned to make a quarrel with me, and get a
week to throw away on some such unknown, inconsiderable slut
as you have been lately lurking with at plays.   150

DORIMANT

Women, when they would break off with a man, never want the
address to turn the fault on him.

MRS LOVEIT

You take a pride of late in using of me ill, that the town may know
the power you have over me, which now (as unreasonably as
yourself) expects that I, do me all the injuries you can, must love   155
you still.

DORIMANT

I am so far from expecting that you should, I begin to think you
never did love me.

MRS LOVEIT

Would the memory of it were so wholly worn out in me that I did
doubt it too. What made you come to disturb my growing quiet?   160

DORIMANT

To give you joy of your growing infamy.

MRS LOVEIT

Insupportable! Insulting devil! This from you, the only author
of my shame! This from another had been but justice, but from
you, 'tis a hellish and inhuman outrage. What have I done?

DORIMANT

A thing that puts you below my scorn and makes my anger as   165
ridiculous as you have made my love.

MRS LOVEIT

I walked last night with Sir Fopling.

DORIMANT

You did, madam; and you talked and laughed aloud, 'Ha, ha,
ha'. Oh, that laugh! That laugh becomes the confidence of a
woman of quality.   170

MRS LOVEIT

You, who have more pleasure in the ruin of a woman's reputation than in the endearments of her love, reproach me not with yourself—and I defy you to name the man can lay a blemish on my fame.

DORIMANT

To be seen publicly so transported with the vain follies of that   175
notorious fop, to me is an infamy below the sin of prostitution with another man.

MRS LOVEIT

Rail on! I am satisfied in the justice of what I did: you had provoked me to it.

DORIMANT

What I did was the effect of a passion whose extravagancies you   180
have been willing to forgive.

MRS LOVEIT

And what I did was the effect of a passion you may forgive if you think fit.

DORIMANT

Are you so indifferent grown?

MRS LOVEIT

I am.   185

DORIMANT

Nay, then 'tis time to part. I'll send you back your letters you have so often asked for. [*Looks in his pockets*] I have two or three of 'em about me.

MRS LOVEIT

Give 'em me.

DORIMANT

You snatch as if you thought I would not. [*Gives her the*   190
letters]—There. And may the perjuries in 'em be mine if e'er I see you more.   *Offers to go: she catches him*

MRS LOVEIT

Stay!

DORIMANT

I will not.

MRS LOVEIT

You shall!   195

DORIMANT

What have you to say?

MRS LOVEIT

I cannot speak it yet.

DORIMANT

Something more in commendation of the fool. Death, I want patience! Let me go.

MRS LOVEIT

I cannot. (*Aside*) I can sooner part with the limbs that hold   200 him.—I hate that nauseous fool, you know I do.

DORIMANT

Was it the scandal you were fond of, then?

MRS LOVEIT

You had raised my anger equal to my love, a thing you ne'er
could do before; and in revenge I did—I know not what I did.
Would you would not think on't any more.   205

DORIMANT

Should I be willing to forget it, I shall be daily minded of it.
'Twill be a commonplace for all the town to laugh at me, and
Medley, when he is rhetorically drunk, will ever be declaiming
on it in my ears.

MRS LOVEIT

'Twill be believed a jealous spite! Come, forget it.   210

DORIMANT

Let me consult my reputation; you are too careless of it. (*Pauses*)
You shall meet Sir Fopling in the Mall again tonight.

MRS LOVEIT

What mean you?

DORIMANT

I have thought on it, and you must. 'Tis necessary to justify my
love to the world. You can handle a coxcomb as he deserves when 215
you are not out of humour, madam.

MRS LOVEIT

Public satisfaction for the wrong I have done you! This is some
new device to make me more ridiculous.

DORIMANT

Hear me.

MRS LOVEIT

I will not.   220

DORIMANT

You will be persuaded.

MRS LOVEIT

Never!

DORIMANT

Are you so obstinate?

MRS LOVEIT

Are you so base?

DORIMANT

You will not satisfy my love?   225

MRS LOVEIT

I would die to satisfy that; but I will not, to save you from a
thousand racks, do a shameless thing to please your vanity.

DORIMANT

Farewell, false woman!

MRS LOVEIT

Do! Go!

DORIMANT

You will call me back again.   230

MRS LOVEIT

Exquisite fiend! I knew you came but to torment me.

Enter BELLINDA *and* PERT

DORIMANT (*surprised*)

Bellinda here!

BELLINDA (*aside*)

He starts and looks pale. The sight of me has touched his guilty soul.

PERT

'Twas but a qualm, as I said, a little indigestion. The surfeit-   235
water did it, madam, mixed with a little mirabilis.

DORIMANT [*aside*]

I am confounded, and cannot guess how she came hither.

MRS LOVEIT

'Tis your fortune, Bellinda, ever to be here when I am abused by this prodigy of ill nature.

BELLINDA

I am amazed to find him here. How has he the face to come near   240
you?

DORIMANT (*aside*)

Here is fine work towards! I never was at such a loss before.

BELLINDA

One who makes a public profession of breach of faith and ingratitude—I loathe the sight of him.

DORIMANT [*aside*]

There is no remedy. I must submit to their tongues now and   245
some other time bring myself off as well as I can.

BELLINDA

Other men are wicked, but then they have some sense of shame. He is never well but when he triumphs—nay, glories—to a woman's face in his villainies.

MRS LOVEIT

You are in the right, Bellinda; but methinks your kindness for   250
me makes you concern yourself too much with him.

36 *mirabilis* aqua mirabilis, a medicinal drink—'The wonderful water, prepared
of cloves, galangols, cubebs, mace, cardomums, nutmegs, ginger, and spirits of
wine, digested twenty-four hours' (Johnson).

48 *glories* Hobbes, *Leviathan* ... (1651) defines 'glory' as '*Joy*, arising from imagination of a mans own power and ability, is that exultation of the mind which is
called GLORYING ...' (pp. 26–7).

BELLINDA

It does indeed, my dear. His barbarous carriage to you yesterday
made me hope you ne'er would see him more, and the very next
day to find him here again provokes me strangely. But because I
know you love him, I have done.   255

DORIMANT

You have reproached me handsomely, and I deserve it for
coming hither, but—

PERT

You must expect it, sir! All women will hate you for my lady's
sake.

DORIMANT [*aside*]

Nay, if she begins too, 'tis time to fly. I shall be scolded to death,   260
else. (*Aside to Bellinda*) I am to blame in some circumstances, I
confess; but as to the main, I am not so guilty as you imagine.
[*Aloud*] I shall seek a more convenient time to clear myself.

MRS LOVEIT

Do it now! What impediments are here?

DORIMANT

I want time, and you want temper.   265

MRS LOVEIT

These are weak pretences!

DORIMANT

You were never more mistaken in your life—and so farewell.

                                              DORIMANT *flings off*

MRS LOVEIT

Call a footman, Pert. Quickly! I will have him dogged.

PERT

I wish you would not, for my quiet and your own.

MRS LOVEIT

I'll find out the infamous causes of all our quarrels, pluck her   270
mask off, and expose her bare-faced to the world!

                                                     [*Exit* PERT]

BELLINDA (*aside*)

Let me but escape this time, I'll never venture more.

MRS LOVEIT

Bellinda, you shall go with me.

BELLINDA

I have such a heaviness hangs on me with what I did this
morning, I would fain go home and sleep, my dear.   275

MRS LOVEIT

Death and eternal darkness! I shall never sleep again. Raging

252 *carriage* behaviour
274 *heaviness* torpor, dullness

fevers seize the world and make mankind as restless all as I am!
Exit MRS LOVEIT

BELLINDA

I knew him false and helped to make him so. Was not her ruin
enough to fright me from the danger? It should have been, but
love can take no warning.   280
Exit BELLINDA

Act V, Scene ii
LADY TOWNLEY's house

Enter MEDLEY, YOUNG BELLAIR, LADY TOWNLEY, EMILIA, and
[SMIRK, a] chaplain

MEDLEY

Bear up, Bellair, and do not let us see that repentance in thine we
daily do in married faces.

LADY TOWNLEY

This wedding will strangely surprise my brother when he knows
it.

MEDLEY

Your nephew ought to conceal it for a time, madam. Since   5
marriage has lost its good name, prudent men seldom expose
their own reputations till 'tis convenient to justify their wives'.

OLD BELLAIR (without)

Where are you all there? Out, adod, will nobody hear?

LADY TOWNLEY

My brother! Quickly, Mr Smirk, into this closet. You must not
be seen yet.   [SMIRK] goes into the closet   10

Enter OLD BELLAIR and LADY TOWNLEY's PAGE

OLD BELLAIR [to PAGE]

Desire Mr Fourbe to walk into the lower parlour. I will be with
him presently.   [Exit PAGE]
(To YOUNG BELLAIR) Where have you been, sir, you could not
wait on me today?

YOUNG BELLAIR

About a business.   15

OLD BELLAIR

Are you so good at business? Adod, I have a business too you
shall dispatch out of hand, sir.—Send for a parson, sister. My
Lady Woodvill and her daughter are coming.

9 closet small inner room for privacy

---

11 Mr Fourbe see note to II.i, 37.

LADY TOWNLEY

What need you huddle up things thus?

OLD BELLAIR

Out a pize! Youth is apt to play the fool, and 'tis not good it   20
should be in their power.

LADY TOWNLEY

You need not fear your son.

OLD BELLAIR

He has been idling this morning, and adod, I do not like him. (*To*
EMILIA)—How dost thou do, sweetheart?

EMILIA

You are very severe, sir. Married in such haste!   25

OLD BELLAIR

Go to, thou'rt a rogue, and I will talk with thee anon. Here's my
Lady Woodvill come.

        Enter LADY WOODVILL, HARRIET, *and* BUSY

Welcome, madam. Mr Fourbe's below with the writings.

LADY WOODVILL

Let us down and make an end, then.

OLD BELLAIR

Sister, show the way. (*To* YOUNG BELLAIR, *who is talking to*   30
HARRIET)—Harry, your business lies not there yet!—Excuse
him till we have done, lady, and then, adod, he shall be for
thee.—Mr Medley, we must trouble you to be a witness.

MEDLEY

I luckily came for that purpose, sir.

        Exeunt OLD BELLAIR, MEDLEY, YOUNG BELLAIR, LADY TOWNLEY,
                and LADY WOODVILL

BUSY [*to* HARRIET]

What will you do, madam?   35

HARRIET

Be carried back and mewed up in the country again, run away
here—anything rather than be married to a man I do not care
for.—Dear Emilia, do thou advise me.

EMILIA

Mr Bellair is engaged, you know.

HARRIET

I do, but know not what the fear of losing an estate may fright   40
him to.

26 *Go to* 'Come along!'
26 *to* V, CA (too Q1)
28 *writings* i.e., the legal documents for the marriage settlement
36 *mewed up* shut up, cooped up

EMILIA

In the desperate condition you are in, you should consult with some judicious man. What think you of Mr Dorimant?

HARRIET

I do not think of him at all.

LUSY [*aside*]

She thinks of nothing else, I am sure.   45

EMILIA

How fond your mother was of Mr Courtage.

HARRIET

Because I contrived the mistake to make a little mirth, you believe I like the man.

EMILIA

Mr Bellair believes you love him.

HARRIET

Men are seldom in the right when they guess at a woman's mind.   50
Would she whom he loves loved him no better!

LUSY (*aside*)

That's e'en well enough, on all conscience.

EMILIA

Mr Dorimant has a great deal of wit.

HARRIET

And takes a great deal of pains to show it.

EMILIA

He's extremely well-fashioned.   55

HARRIET

Affectedly grave, or ridiculously wild and apish.

LUSY

You defend him still against your mother.

HARRIET

I would not, were he justly rallied; but I cannot hear anyone undeservedly railed at.

EMILIA

Has your woman learnt the song you were so taken with?   60

HARRIET

I was fond of a new thing. 'Tis dull at second hearing.

EMILIA

Mr Dorimant made it.

LUSY

She knows it, madam, and has made me sing it at least a dozen times this morning.

HARRIET

Thy tongue is as impertinent as thy fingers.   65

56 *wild and apish* for 'wild' see Introduction, pp. xxix–xxxi. 'Apish' meant either ape-like, or foolishly imitative like an ape.

EMILIA [*to* BUSY]
  You have provoked her.
BUSY
  'Tis but singing the song and I shall appease her.
EMILIA
  Prithee, do.
HARRIET
  She has a voice will grate your ears worse than a catcall, and
  dresses so ill she's scarce fit to trick up a yeoman's daughter on a   7(
  holiday.

BUSY *sings*
Song, by Sir C. S.

As Amoret with Phillis sat
  One evening on the plain,
And saw the charming Strephon wait
  To tell the nymph his pain,   7.

The threat'ning danger to remove,
  She whispered in her ear,
'Ah, Phillis, if you would not love,
  This shepherd do not hear:

None ever had so strange an art,   8(
  His passion to convey
Into a list'ning virgin's heart
  And steal her soul away.

Fly, fly betimes, for fear you give
  Occasion for your fate'.   8!
'In vain', said she, 'in vain I strive.
  Alas, 'tis now too late'.

---

84 *betimes* in good time

69 *catcall* a kind of whistle. On 7 March 1660 Pepys went to Pope's Head Alley and
   'bought a catcall there, it cost me two groats'. Certainly it was used later in the
   century and in the eighteenth-century theatre to demonstrate an audience's
   disapproval. See Leo Hughes, *The Drama's Patrons* (Austin and London,
   1971), pp. 35–43.
71 s.d. *Sir C.S.* almost certainly by Sir Car Scroope who wrote the prologue,
   rather than Sir Charles Sedley to whom it was attributed in 1722. Brett-Smith
   supplies the lines from an elegy by Comtesse de la Suze in the *Recueil des Pièces
   Gallantes* which Scroope imitated. It was an unusually popular song, and
   appears in several manuscripts, musical broadsides, and songbooks (Thorpe,
   p. 144).

Enter DORIMANT

DORIMANT
        'Music so softens and disarms the mind—'
HARRIET
        'That not one arrow does resistance find'.
DORIMANT
    Let us make use of the lucky minute, then.   90
HARRIET (*aside, turning from* DORIMANT)
    My love springs with my blood into my face. I dare not look upon
    him yet.
DORIMANT
    What have we here—the picture of a celebrated beauty giving
    audience in public to a declared lover?
HARRIET
    Play the dying fop and make the piece complete, sir.   95
DORIMANT
    What think you if the hint were well improved—the whole
    mystery of making love pleasantly designed and wrought in a suit
    of hangings?
HARRIET
    'Twere needless to execute fools in effigy who suffer daily in
    their own persons.   100
DORIMANT (*to* EMILIA, *aside*)
    Mistress Bride, for such I know this happy day has made you—
EMILIA
    Defer the formal joy you are to give me, and mind your business
    with her. (*Aloud*)—Here are dreadful preparations, Mr Dorim-
    ant—writings sealing, and a parson sent for.
DORIMANT
    To marry this lady?   105
BUSY
    Condemned she is; and what will become of her I know not,
    without you generously engage in a rescue.
DORIMANT
    In this sad condition, madam, I can do no less than offer you my
    service.

93 *a celebrated* B, CA, CO (celebrated Q1; Brett-Smith believes 'a' was acciden-
        tally omitted and notes the parallelism with 'a declared lover' in l. 94)
97–8 *suit of hangings* set of tapestry wall-hangings
101 *Mistress* ed. (Mrs. Q1)

88–9 *Music . . . find* Waller, 'Of my Lady Isabella, Playing on the Lute', ll. 11–12
    (*Poems*, ed. G. Thorn Drury (1901), vol. 1, 90), but with 'one' substituted for
    'an'.

HARRIET

The obligation is not great; you are the common sanctuary for all   110
young women who run from their relations.

DORIMANT

I have always my arms open to receive the distressed. But I will
open my heart and receive you where none yet did ever enter.
You have filled it with a secret, might I but let you know it—

HARRIET

Do not speak it if you would have me believe it. Your tongue is so   115
famed for falsehood, 'twill do the truth an injury.

Turns away her head

DORIMANT

Turn not away, then, but look on me and guess it.

HARRIET

Did you not tell me there was no credit to be given to faces—that
women nowadays have their passions as much at will as they have
their complexions, and put on joy and sadness, scorn and kind-   120
ness, with the same ease they do their paint and patches? Are
they the only counterfeits?

DORIMANT

You wrong your own while you suspect my eyes. By all the hope
I have in you, the inimitable colour in your cheeks is not more
free from art than are the sighs I offer.   125

HARRIET

In men who have been long hardened in sin, we have reason to
mistrust the first signs of repentance.

DORIMANT

The prospect of such a heaven will make me persevere and give
you marks that are infallible.

HARRIET

What are those?   130

DORIMANT

I will renounce all the joys I have in friendship and wine,
sacrifice to you all the interest I have in other women—

HARRIET

Hold! Though I wish you devout, I would not have you turn
fanatic. Could you neglect these a while and make a journey into
the country?   135

DORIMANT

To be with you, I could live there and never send one thought to
London.

HARRIET

Whate'er you say, I know all beyond Hyde Park's a desert to you,
and that no gallantry can draw you farther.

DORIMANT

That has been the utmost limit of my love; but now my passion   140
knows no bounds, and there's no measure to be taken of what I'll
do for you from anything I ever did before.

HARRIET

When I hear you talk thus in Hampshire, I shall begin to think
there may be some little truth enlarged upon.

DORIMANT

Is this all? Will you not promise me—   145

HARRIET

I hate to promise! What we do then is expected from us and
wants much of the welcome it finds when it surprises.

DORIMANT

May I not hope?

HARRIET

That depends on you and not on me; and 'tis to no purpose to
forbid it.   *Turns to* BUSY   150

BUSY

Faith, madam, now I perceive the gentleman loves you too. E'en
let him know your mind, and torment yourselves no longer.

HARRIET

Dost think I have no sense of modesty?

BUSY

Think, if you lose this, you may never have another opportunity.

HARRIET

May he hate me—a curse that frights me when I speak it!—if   155
ever I do a thing against the rules of decency and honour.

DORIMANT (*to* EMILIA)

I am beholding to you for your good intentions, madam.

EMILIA

I thought the concealing of our marriage from her might have
done you better service.

DORIMANT

Try her again.   160

EMILIA [*to* HARRIET]

What have you resolved, madam? The time draws near.

HARRIET

To be obstinate and protest against this marriage.

Enter LADY TOWNLEY *in haste*

LADY TOWNLEY (*to* EMILIA)

Quickly, quickly, let Mr Smirk out of the closet!

SMIRK *comes out of the closet*

144 *little* Q1ᶜ (*omitted* Q1ᵘ, W, V)

HARRIET

A parson! [*To* DORIMANT]—Had you laid him in here?

DORIMANT

I knew nothing of him.   165

HARRIET

Should it appear you did, your opinion of my easiness may cost you dear.

Enter OLD BELLAIR, YOUNG BELLAIR, MEDLEY, *and* LADY WOODVILL

OLD BELLAIR

Out a pize, the canonical hour is almost past! Sister, is the man of God come?

LADY TOWNLEY [*indicating* SMIRK]

He waits your leisure.   170

OLD BELLAIR [*to* SMIRK]

By your favour, sir—Adod, a pretty spruce fellow! What may we call him?

LADY TOWNLEY

Mr Smirk—my Lady Biggot's chaplain.

OLD BELLAIR

A wise woman, adod she is! The man will serve for the flesh as well as the spirit.—Please you, sir, to commission a young   175 couple to go to bed together a God's name?—Harry!

YOUNG BELLAIR

Here, sir.

OLD BELLAIR

Out a pize! Without your mistress in your hand?

SMIRK

Is this the gentleman?

OLD BELLAIR

Yes, sir.   180

SMIRK

Are you not mistaken, sir?

OLD BELLAIR

Adod, I think not, sir!

SMIRK

Sure you are, sir.

OLD BELLAIR

You look as if you would forbid the banns, Mr Smirk. I hope you have no pretension to the lady!   185

176 *a* Q1 (i' V)

___

166 *easiness* see note to I, 119.
168 *canonical hour* the hours in which marriage could take place legally (8–12 a.m.).

SMIRK

Wish him joy, sir! I have done him the good office today already.

OLD BELLAIR

Out a pize! What do I hear?

LADY TOWNLEY

Never storm, brother. The truth is out.

OLD BELLAIR

How say you, sir? Is this your wedding day?

YOUNG BELLAIR

It is, sir.   190

OLD BELLAIR

And, adod, it shall be mine too. (*To* EMILIA) Give me thy hand, sweetheart. [*She refuses*] What dost thou mean? Give me thy hand, I say!   EMILIA *kneels, and* YOUNG BELLAIR

LADY TOWNLEY

Come, come, give her your blessing. This is the woman your son loved and is married to.   195

OLD BELLAIR

Ha! Cheated! Cozened! And by your contrivance, sister!

LADY TOWNLEY

What would you do with her? She's a rogue, and you can't abide her.

MEDLEY

Shall I hit her a pat for you, sir?

OLD BELLAIR

Adod, you are all rogues, and I never will forgive you.   200
                                   [*Flings away, as if to exit*]

LADY TOWNLEY

Whither? Whither away?

MEDLEY

Let him go and cool awhile.

LADY WOODVILL (*to* DORIMANT)

Here's a business broke out now, Mr Courtage. I am made a fine fool of.

DORIMANT

You see the old gentleman knew nothing of it.   205

LADY WOODVILL

I find he did not. I shall have some trick put upon me, if I stay in this wicked town any longer.—Harriet, dear child, where art thou? I'll into the country straight.

OLD BELLAIR

Adod, madam, you shall hear me first—

Enter MRS LOVEIT *and* BELLINDA

196 *Cozened* defrauded, duped

MRS LOVEIT
Hither my m. n dogged him.   210

BELLINDA
Yonder he sta 1s, my dear.

MRS LOVEIT
I see him, (*aside*) and with him the face that has undone me. Oh,
that I were but where I might throw out the anguish of my heart!
Here it must rage within and break ʲt.

LADY TOWNLEY
Mrs Loveit! Aʲ you afraid to come forward?   215

MRS LOVEIT
I was amazed to see so much company here in a morning. The
occasion sure is extraordinary.

DORIMANT (*aside*)
Loveit and Bellinda! The devil owes me a shame today, and I
think never will h ve done paying it.

MRS LOVEIT
Married! Dear Emilia, how am I transported with the news!   220

HARRIET (*to* DORIMANT)
I little thought Emilia was the woman Mr Bellair was in love
with. I'll chide her for not trusting me with the secret.

DORIMANT
How do you like Mrs Loveit?

HARRIET
She's a famed mistress of yours, I hear.

DORIMANT
She has been, on occasion.   225

OLD BELLAIR (*to* LADY WOODVILL)
Adod, madam, I cannot help it.

LADY WOODVILL
You need make no more apologies, sir.

EMILIA (*to* MRS LOVEIT)
The old gentleman's excusing himself to my Lady Woodvill.

MRS LOVEIT
Ha, ha, ha! I never heard of anything so pleasant.

HARRIET (*to* DORIMANT)
She's extremely overjoyed at something.   230

DORIMANT
At nothing. She is one of those hoiting ladies who gaily fling

224 *mistress* V, CA (Mrs. Q1)
231 *hoiting* involved in riotous and noisy mirth, acting the hoyden

218–19 *The devil . . . it* Carnochan points out that Dorimant varies the proverb, 'the
devil owed (one) a shame and now has paid it' (Tilley, op. cit., pp. 152–3).

themselves about and force a laugh when their aching hearts are
full of discontent and malice.

MRS LOVEIT

Oh heaven! I was never so near killing myself with laughing.—Mr Dorimant, are you a brideman?   235

LADY WOODVILL

Mr Dorimant! Is this Mr Dorimant, madam?

MRS LOVEIT

If you doubt it, your daughter can resolve you, I suppose.

LADY WOODVILL

I am cheated too, basely cheated!

OLD BELLAIR

Out a pize, what's here? More knavery yet?

LADY WOODVILL

Harriet! On my blessing, come away, I charge you.   240

HARRIET

Dear mother, do but stay and hear me.

LADY WOODVILL

I am betrayed, and thou art undone, I fear.

HARRIET

Do not fear it. I have not, nor never will, do anything against my
duty. Believe me, dear mother, do!

DORIMANT (*to* MRS LOVEIT)

I had trusted you with this secret but that I knew the violence of   245
your nature would ruin my fortune—as now unluckily it has. I
thank you, madam.

MRS LOVEIT

She's an heiress, I know, and very rich.

DORIMANT

To satisfy you, I must give up my interest wholly to my love.
Had you been a reasonable woman, I might have secured 'em   250
both and been happy.

MRS LOVEIT

You might have trusted me with anything of this kind, you know
you might. Why did you go under a wrong name?

DORIMANT

The story is too long to tell you now. Be satisfied; this is the
business, this is the mask has kept me from you.   255

BELLINDA (*aside*)

He's tender of my honour, though he's cruel to my love.

MRS LOVEIT

Was it no idle mistress, then?

DORIMANT

Believe me—a wife, to repair the ruins of my estate that needs
it.

MRS LOVEIT

The knowledge of this makes my grief hang lighter on my soul,
but I shall never more be happy.   260

DORIMANT

Bellinda—

BELLINDA

Do not think of clearing yourself with me. It is impossible. Do all
men break their words thus?

DORIMANT

Th' extravagant words they speak in love. 'Tis as unreasonable to
expect we should perform all we promise then, as do all we   265
threaten when we are angry. When I see you next—

BELLINDA

Take no notice of me, and I shall not hate you.

DORIMANT

How came you to Mrs Loveit?

BELLINDA

By a mistake the chairmen made for want of my giving them
directions.   270

DORIMANT

'Twas a pleasant one. We must meet again.

BELLINDA

Never.

DORIMANT

Never?

BELLINDA

When we do, may I be as infamous as you are false.

LADY TOWNLEY

Men of Mr Dorimant's character always suffer in the general   275
opinion of the world.

MEDLEY

You can make no judgment of a witty man from common fame,
considering the prevailing faction, madam.

OLD BELLAIR

Adod, he's in the right.

273 *Never?* V, CA (Never! Q1)

278 *prevailing faction* antipathy to the Wits, and the Wits' defensive reaction, is
   evident in Dryden's dedication of *The Assignation* (1673) to Sir Charles Sedley,
   which speaks of 'the ignorant and ridiculous Descriptions which some Pedants
   have given of the Wits (as they are pleas'd to call them) . . . those wretches Paint
   leudness, Atheism, Folly, ill-Reasoning, and all manner of Extravagances
   amongst us, for want of understanding what we are' (*Dramatic Works*, ed. M.
   Summers (1931–32), vol. 3, 276). (Cited by Conaghan.)

MEDLEY

Besides, 'tis a common error among women to believe too well of   280
them they know and too ill of them they don't.

OLD BELLAIR

Adod, he observes well.

LADY TOWNLEY

Believe me, madam, you will find Mr Dorimant as civil a
gentleman as you thought Mr Courtage.

HARRIET

If you would but know him better—   285

LADY WOODVILL

You have a mind to know him better? Come away! You shall
never see him more.

HARRIET

Dear mother, stay!

LADY WOODVILL

I won't be consenting to your ruin.

HARRIET

Were my fortune in your power—   290

LADY WOODVILL

Your person is.

HARRIET

Could I be disobedient, I might take it out of yours and put it
into his.

LADY WOODVILL

'Tis that you would be at! You would marry this Dorimant!

HARRIET

I cannot deny it. I would, and never will marry any other man.   295

LADY WOODVILL

Is this the duty that you promised?

HARRIET

But I will never marry him against your will.

LADY WOODVILL (aside)

She knows the way to melt my heart. (To HARRIET)—Upon
yourself light your undoing.

MEDLEY (to OLD BELLAIR)

Come, sir, you have not the heart any longer to refuse your   300
blessing.

OLD BELLAIR

Adod, I ha' not.—Rise, and God bless you both! Make much of
her, Harry; she deserves thy kindness. (To EMILIA) Adod, sirrah,
I did not think it had been in thee.

Enter SIR FOPLING *and his* PAGE

SIR FOPLING

'Tis a damned windy day. Hey, page! Is my periwig right?   305

PAGE

A little out of order, sir.

SIR FOPLING

Pox o' this apartment! It wants an antechamber to adjust one's self in. (*To* MRS LOVEIT)—Madam, I came from your house, and your servants directed me hither.

MRS LOVEIT

I will give order hereafter they shall direct you better.   310

SIR FOPLING

The great satisfaction I had in the Mall last night has given me much disquiet since.

MRS LOVEIT

'Tis likely to give me more than I desire.

SIR FOPLING [*aside*]

What the devil makes her so reserved?—Am I guilty of an indiscretion, madam?   315

MRS LOVEIT

You will be of a great one, if you continue your mistake, sir.

SIR FOPLING

Something puts you out of humour.

MRS LOVEIT

The most foolish, inconsiderable thing that ever did.

SIR FOPLING

Is it in my power?

MRS LOVEIT

To hang or drown it. Do one of 'em, and trouble me no more.   320

SIR FOPLING

So *fière*? *Serviteur*, madam!—Medley, where's Dorimant?

MEDLEY

Methinks the lady has not made you those advances today she did last night, Sir Fopling.

SIR FOPLING

Prithee, do not talk of her.

MEDLEY

She would be a *bonne fortune*.   325

SIR FOPLING

Not to me at present.

MEDLEY

How so?

307–8 *one's self* ed. (ones self Q1; oneself V, CA)
321 *fière* proud, haughty
321 *Serviteur* your servant

SIR FOPLING
  An intrigue now would be but a temptation to me to throw away
  that vigour on one which I mean shall shortly make my court to
  the whole sex in a ballet.   330
MEDLEY
  Wisely considered, Sir Fopling.
SIR FOPLING
  No one woman is worth the loss of a cut in a caper.
MEDLEY
  Not when 'tis so universally designed.
LADY WOODVILL
  Mr Dorimant, everyone has spoke so much in your behalf that I
  can no longer doubt but I was in the wrong.   335
MRS LOVEIT [*to* BELLINDA]
  There's nothing but falsehood and impertinence in this world.
  All men are villains or fools. Take example from my misfor-
  tunes. Bellinda, if thou wouldst be happy, give thyself wholly up
  to goodness.
HARRIET (*to* MRS LOVEIT)
  Mr Dorimant has been your God Almighty long enough. 'Tis 340
  time to think of another.
MRS LOVEIT [*to* BELLINDA]
  Jeered by her! I will lock myself up in my house and never see the
  world again.
HARRIET
  A nunnery is the more fashionable place for such a retreat and
  has been the fatal consequence of many a *belle passion*.   345
MRS LOVEIT [*aside*]
  Hold, heart, till I get home! Should I answer, 'twould make her
  triumph greater.   *Is going out*
DORIMANT
  Your hand, Sir Fopling—
SIR FOPLING
  Shall I wait upon you, madam?
MRS LOVEIT
  Legion of fools, as many devils take thee!   *Exit* MRS LOVEIT 350
MEDLEY
  Dorimant! I pronounce thy reputation clear, and henceforward,

337–8 *misfortunes. Bellinda*, Q1 (misfortunes, Bellinda; V, B)
345 *belle passion* violent passion

332 *cut* a step in dancing (*OED* gives this as its first example). From the verb 'cut',
  to spring into the air and kick the feet with great rapidity (current from 1603).
350 *Legion* innumerable hosts, with an echo of Mark v. 9, 'My name *is* Legion for we
  are many'. Cf. Epilogue, l. 18.

when I would know anything of woman, I will consult no other
oracle.

SIR FOPLING

Stark mad, by all that's handsome!—Dorimant, thou hast
engaged me in a pretty business.   355

DORIMANT

I have not leisure now to talk about it.

OLD BELLAIR

Out a pize, what does this man of mode do here again?

LADY TOWNLEY

He'll be an excellent entertainment within, brother, and is luckily come to raise the mirth of the company.

LADY WOODVILL

Madam, I take my leave of you.   360

LADY TOWNLEY

What do you mean, madam?

LADY WOODVILL

To go this afternoon part of my way to Hartley—

OLD BELLAIR

Adod, you shall stay and dine first! Come, we will all be good
friends, and you shall give Mr Dorimant leave to wait upon you
and your daughter in the country.   365

LADY WOODVILL

If his occasions bring him that way, I have now so good an
opinion of him, he shall be welcome.

HARRIET

To a great, rambling, lone house that looks as it were not
inhabited, the family's so small. There you'll find my mother, an
old lame aunt, and myself, sir, perched up on chairs at a distance 370
in a large parlour, sitting moping like three or four melancholy
birds in a spacious volary. Does not this stagger your resolution?

DORIMANT

Not at all, madam. The first time I saw you, you left me with the
pangs of love upon me, and this day my soul has quite given up
her liberty.   375

HARRIET

This is more dismal than the country.—Emilia, pity me who am
going to that sad place. Methinks I hear the hateful noise of rooks

366 *occasions* 1) needs, requirements, 2) affairs, business

---

362 *Hartley* there are a Hartley Wespall, a Hartley Mauditt, and a Hartley Wintney
in Hampshire.

372 *volary* a large bird-cage; an aviary. Introduced from the French *volière* in the
seventeenth century. *OED* cites first instance from Jonson's *New Inn* (1630),
V.i.

already—kaw, kaw, kaw. There's music in the worst cry in
London—'My dill and cucumbers to pickle'.

OLD BELLAIR

Sister, knowing of this matter, I hope you have provided us some   380
good cheer.

LADY TOWNLEY

I have, brother, and the fiddles too.

OLD BELLAIR

Let 'em strike up then. The young lady shall have a dance before
she departs.   *Dance*
(*After the dance*) So now we'll in, and make this an arrant   385
wedding day.
(*To the pit*)
            And if these honest gentlemen rejoice,
            Adod, the boy has made a happy choice.

                                                    Exeunt omnes

---

379 *My dill ... pickle* Addison, writing on the cries of London street-traders, 'I am
always pleased with that particular Time of the Year which is proper for the
pickling of Dill and Cucumbers; but alas this Cry, like the Song of the
Nightingales, is not heard above two Months' (*The Spectator*, No. 251 (18 Dec.
1711)).

THE EPILOGUE
By Mr Dryden

Most modern wits such monstrous fools have shown,
They seemed not of heav'n's making, but their own.
Those nauseous harlequins in farce may pass,
But there goes more to a substantial ass!
Something of man must be exposed to view,   5
That, gallants, it may more resemble you.
Sir Fopling is a fool so nicely writ,
The ladies would mistake him for a wit,
And when he sings, talks loud, and cocks, would cry:
'I vow, methinks, he's pretty company—   10
So brisk, so gay, so travelled, so refined!'
As he took pains to graft upon his kind,
True fops help nature's work, and go to school
To file and finish God A'mighty's fool.
Yet none Sir Fopling him, or him, can call—   15
He's knight o' the shire and represents ye all.
From each he meets, he culls whate'er he can:
Legion's his name, a people in a man.

6 *it* B, CA (they Q1; Brett-Smith adopts text from Bodleian ms.: see Note on
   Text)
9 *cocks* struts, brags, or crows over
10 *I vow* Q1 (I now B; Aye, now CA; both readings follow ms. text)
11 *refined!'* ed. (refin'd! Q1; refined, CA; V regards l. 11 as the only line cried out
   by the ladies)
12 *upon ... kind* upon what nature gave him
12 *kind,* ed. (kind. Q1; kind.' CA)
12–14 Sloane ms. adds an extra couplet after l. 12: 'Labouring to put in more as
   Mr. Bayes/Thrums in Additions to his ten yeares playes'. Bodleian ms. places
   the couplet, with slight variants, after l. 14. (Further, see Note on Tèxt)
16 *knight o' the shire* parliamentary representative of a shire (or county)

3 *harlequins* Harlequin is the traditional figure in French and Italian farce.
   Travelling companies from the continent had been well received in England,
   but were disapproved of by Dryden (and later Pope) as a vulgar, 'low' form.
12–14 See textual note. Dryden's additional couplet 'turns the tables on George
   Villiers, Duke of Buckingham, for his satiric portrait of Dryden as Bayes in *The
   Rehearsal*; Buckingham's play was several years in the making before its first
   appearance in 1671 and was often amended afterward' (Carnochan).
18 *Legion* see note to V.ii, 350.

His bulky folly gathers as it goes,
And, rolling o'er you, like a snowball grows.   20
His various modes from various fathers follow;
One taught the toss, and one the new French wallow.
His sword-knot, this, his cravat, this designed —
And this, the yard-long snake he twirls behind.
From one, the sacred periwig he gained,   25
Which wind ne'er blew, nor touch of hat profaned;
Another's diving bow he did adore,
Which with a shog casts all the hair before,
Till he with full decorum brings it back
And rises with a water spaniel shake.   30
As for his songs (the ladies' dear delight),
Those sure he took from most of you who write.
Yet every man is safe from what he feared,
For no one fool is hunted from the herd.

21 *modes* see note to II. ii, 29.
22 *toss* i.e., of the head. *OED* gives as first example of this usage.
22 *wallow* rolling walk or gait. *OED* gives this sole example
24 *snake* long curl or tail attached to a wig. *OED* gives this example, and one from
    Swift (1728).
26 *nor ... profaned* for the fashion of carrying the hat (to avoid disordering the
    wig), cf. Dryden's 'Epilogue Spoken at the Opening of the New House', l. 13,
    'So may your Hats your Foretops never press ...'
28 *shog* shake, jerk. Cotgrave (1611) gives 'shake, shog, or shocke' as synonyms.
33–4 *Yet ... herd* a conventional claim, but although identifications were quickly
    made, Dryden's claim is probably correct (see Introduction, pp. xiii–xv,
    xvii–xx).

APPENDIX A

DR STAGGINS'S SETTINGS OF DORIMANT'S SONG AND SIR CAR SCROOPE'S SONG

These two settings of Dorimant's song ('When first Amintas charmed my heart') in Act III, Scene i, and Sir Car Scroope's song ('As Amoret with Phiilis sat') in Act V, Scene ii, are the nearest contemporary settings known. Dr Nicholas Staggins (1650?–1700) was made master of 'his Majesty's Music' in 1675, but he published few of his compositions.

The nearest contemporary setting of Sir Fopling's song (Act IV, Scene ii) dates from 1707, and is by Ramonden (see Thorpe, pp. 103–104).

Mr Philip Wilby has kindly made these modern realizations from the original printed music. The part for the piano, which would have been improvised at will, has been added by Mr Wilby.

Staggins's setting of Dorimant's song is printed in John Playford's *Choice Ayres and Songs to sing to the Theorbo-Lute, or Bass-Viol: being most of the Newest Ayres and Songs Sung at Court, And at the Publick Theatres. Composed by Several Gentlemen of His Majesty's Music, and Others ... The Fifth Book* (1684), p. 38. Ramonden's setting, dating from 1707, is also extant. For a record of other printings of the song, and reprintings of Staggins's music, see Thorpe, p. 102.

Staggins's setting of Sir Car Scroope's song is printed in Playford's *Choice Ayres ... The Second Book* (1679), p. 5. It was an unusually popular song. Thorpe (p. 144) records manuscript copies, various printings, and further notes that its popularity continued into the early eighteenth century.

'When First Amintas Charmed My Heart'

When first A-min-tas charmed my heart, My

heed-less sheep be-gan to stray; The wolves soon stole the

great-est part, And all will now be made a prey.

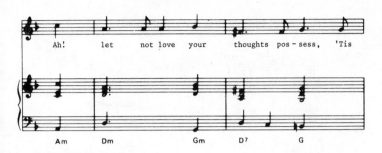

Ah! let not love your thoughts pos-sess, 'Tis

Am Dm Gm D7 G

fa - tal to a shep-herd-ess; The dan-g'-rous pas-sion

A7 Dm Gm Gm C C F Cm7 F

you must shun, Or else like me be quite un-done.

G7 A7 Dm Gm A Dm Gm G Asup4 3 Dm

SIR GEORGE ETHEREGE

'As Amoret with Phillis Sat'

VOICE

As A - mor-et with Phil - lis sat, One

PIANO

GUITAR   Gm   Gm   Eb   Cm   D

even - ing on the plain, And saw the charm-ing

C(m)   Gm   Cm   D7   Gm   Cm   F7

Stre - phon wait to tell the nymph his pain, The

Bb   F   Eb   F7   Bb

threat'-ning dan-ger to re-move, She whis-pered in her

ear, Ah Phil-lis, if you would not love

This shep-herd do not hear, This shep-herd do not hear.

APPENDIX B

THE BULLIES' SONG

The scraps of the song directed by the bullies at Sir Fopling, Mrs Loveit, and Bellinda in Act III, Scene iii, 202, 211 have been identified by W. B. Carnochan as being from an anonymous ballad in *A New Collection of the Choicest Songs. Now in Esteem in Town or Court* (1676), sig. B6ᵛ. The volume also contains Dorimant's song ('When first Amintas'), mistakenly attributed to Sir Fopling, the drinking-song from Act IV, Scene i, and Sir Car Scroope's song. The song sung by the bullies became the basis for a ballad, 'Love al-a-Mode, or, the Modish Mistris' (Pepys Collection, iii. 102; Pepysian Library, Magdalene College, Cambridge). The text in *A New Collection*, which has no musical setting, is as follows:

> Tell me no more you love,
>   Unless you will grant my desire,
> Ev'rything else will prove,
>   But fuel to my fire.
>
> 'Tis not for kisses alone,
>   So long I have made my address,
> There's some thing else to be done,
>   Which you cannot chuse but guess.
>
> 'Tis not a charming smile,
>   That brings me the perfect Joys,
> Nor can you me beguile,
>   With sighs and with languishing eyes:
>
> There is an essence within,
>   Kind Nature hath clear'd the doubt,
> Such bliss can never be sin,
>   And therefore i'le find it out.

Set, printed and bound in Great Britain by
Cox & Wyman Ltd
London, Fakenham and Reading